Sept

W9-BOZ-022

SONGS
THAT LIFT
THE HEART

A Personal Story by

GEORGE BEVERLY SHEA

with Fred Bauer

CRUSADE EDITION

Published by

World Wide Publications

1313 Hennepin Avenue

Minneapolis, Minnesota 55403

Scripture references in this volume are from the *King James Version of the Bible.*

Grateful acknowledgment is extended to those who made it possible to include the music and words of the hymns in this volume.

Used by permission of the Chancel Music Company: "Adoration" by Mrs. A. J. Shea, copyright 1947 by George Beverly Shea, © 1965 by Chancel Music Co.; "Blue Galilee" by George Beverly Shea, copyright 1947 by George Beverly Shea, assigned to Hope Publishing Company; "I'd Rather Have Jesus" by Rhea F. Miller and George Beverly Shea, copyright 1922 Rhea F. Miller, copyright renewal 1950, copyright 1939 George Beverly Shea, renewal 1966, assigned to Chancel Music Inc., international copyright secured (BMI); "I Will Praise Him" by George Beverly Shea © 1971 by Chancel Music Inc. (BMI) international copyright secured; "Let Not Your Heart Be Troubled" by Arthur Smith and George Beverly Shea, © copyright 1970 by Chancel Music Inc.; "Songs in the Night" by J. Thurston Noé and Dr. Will Houghton, © copyright assigned to Chancel Music, Inc.

"The Wonder of It All" by George Beverly Shea © 1956 by Chancel Music, Inc. International copyright secured.

Used by permission of Fiesta Music Inc.: "I Found What I Wanted" by Ralph Carmichael.

Used by permission of Hope Publishing Company: "Singing I Go" by E. E. Hewitt and William J. Kirkpatrick; "Have Thine Own Way" by Adelaide A. Pollard and George Stebbins; "The Christ of Every Road" by Dr. Will Houghton and Wendell P. Loveless; "Songs in the Night" by Wendell P. Loveless; "He Will Hold Me Fast" by Ada R. Habershon and Robert Harkness.

Used by permission of the Lynn Music Corporation: "Acres of Diamonds" by Arthur Smith and Robert Harkness. © Copyright 1959 by Lynn Music Corp., P.O. Box 153, Brewster, N.Y. International Copyright Secured. All Rights Reserved.

Used by permission of the Rodeheaver Co.: "The Old Rugged Cross" by George Bennard, Copyright 1913 by George Bennard. The Rodeheaver Co., Owner. Renewed 1941 (extended); "Then Jesus Came" by Oswald J. Smith and Homer Rodeheaver, Copyright 1940 by the Rodeheaver Co. © Renewed 1968.

All Rights Reserved; "Beyond the Sunset" by Virgil and Blanche Brock, Copyright 1936 by the Rodeheaver Co. © Renewed 1964. All Rights Reserved; "Speak My Lord" by George Bennard. Copyright 1911 by George Bennard. Renewed 1939 (extended), by George Bennard. Assigned to the Rodeheaver Co.

Used by permission of G. Schirmer, Inc.: "Thou Light of Light" by J. Thurston Noé, Copyright 1958 by G. Schirmer, Inc.

The quoted material from *Streams in the Desert* by Mrs. Charles E. Cowman is copyrighted by Cowman Publications, Inc., of Grand Rapids, Michigan, and is used by permission of Zondervan Publishing House.

The article by Glenn D. Kittler from *Guideposts,* © 1964 Guideposts Associated, Carmel, N.Y., is used by permission.

Reminiscences and Gospel Hymn Stories by George Stebbins, Copyright 1924, George H. Doran Company. Used by permission of Doubleday and Co., Inc.

Used by permission of the Malvern Music Company: "If You Know the Lord" by Bickley Reichner. Copyright 1951 Malvern Music Company.

Used by permission of Manna Music Inc.: "How Great Thou Art" by Carl Boberg, translated by Stuart K. Hine, © Copyright 1955 by Manna Music Inc., North Hollywood, California. International Copyright Secured. All Rights Reserved.

Used by permission of the Nazarene Publishing House: "The Love of God" by F. M. Lehman. Copyright 1917 and 1945 by Nazarene Publishing House.

Used by permission of Hill and Range Songs, Inc.: "It Took a Miracle" by John Peterson, Copyright 1948 by Percy B. Crawford. Copyright assigned to Hill and Range Songs, Inc.

"Oh, How Sweet It Is to Know" by Cindy Walker, Copyright © 1955 by Hill and Range Songs, Inc.

Table of Contents

Foreword

One of the requisites for working on a book with George Beverly Shea is a sturdy suitcase. The reason is that this twenty-five-year veteran of Billy Graham Crusades is a man in perpetual motion. When we collaborated on *Then Sings My Soul,* his autobiography, I followed him from his headquarters just outside of Chicago ("Just a stone's throw from my second home, Chicago's O'Hare Airport," he jokes), to San Juan, Puerto Rico, to New York, to West Palm Beach, Florida, back to the Shea home and finally East where we spent three days together in my home in Princeton, New Jersey, and another marathon day in a New York City hotel room, checking galley proofs just before the book went off to press — and just before my peripatetic friend went off on another singing mission.

The preparation of this book has required no less traveling on my part, though it has been limited primarily to excursions between New York and Chicago. One trip to Nashville to meet Bev and another with him to Ottawa, Canada, were exceptions. (On my way home from Canada, I visited Bev's ninety-year-old mother in Syracuse.) I did consider trailing Bev to the Holy Land, Rome, and Australia in the spring, but a look at his jampacked schedule convinced me we would make little progress on the manuscript, so I stayed behind compiling and weaving together the material that we already had agreed should be included. Questions that I had or new thoughts, additions, or corrections from him were passed back and forth in the mails.

To paraphrase a popular TV commercial, someone might ask: Is this any way to write a book? My response would be: With George Beverly Shea, it is the only way. Waiting for him to come stationary, sit down to a typewriter and pore over it for the months it takes to prepare a manuscript, would simply mean that a book would not be forthcoming. Therefore, we have worked out an alternative, a catch-as-catch-can procedure which in at least one previous effort produced favorable enough results that we were encouraged to try again.

There was one junket which I should like to elaborate upon. That was to Nashville in February where I sat in on the recording of Bev's thirty-sixth RCA album, *Amazing Grace*. I must tell you about this experience, for it is fresh in mind and will serve as well as anything to paint the personality of this much-admired man. Traveling about with him, being with him on the platform, associating with his friends on the Billy Graham team, coming to know his lovely wife, Erma, and his fine son and daughter, Ron and Lainie, corresponding with him, sharing some of his joys and disappointments, watching and listening to the people who have been blessed by his singing, I have come to understand the veneration people all over the world have for him. He is worthy of it, but I might add — unaffected by it.

Without doubt, he is one of the most humble men I've ever been around. People who have known Bev from "the early days" say he is still the same fellow who unassumingly and somewhat shyly played the organ in his father's church; the same young man who worked in a New York life insurance company and sang on the side; the same modest announcer who worked for a Chicago radio station; the same quiet, dignified gospel hymn singer Billy Graham sought out when he began his world-wide ministry.

But most of the people I've mentioned are of a religious persuasion and most of the settings of a spiritual tone. I wondered as I flew into Nashville, considered by many to be the music capital of the country, how Bev would respond to a more secular milieu, how he would be accepted in an arena where the purveyors of musical talent often talk in terms of top billing, top forty, Gold records, showmanship, color, marketability — terms many would consider incongruous with sacred music.

I should not have been surprised to find Bev the same as always. The people around him — top names in popular music, but not necessarily strangers to gospel music — greeted him with genuine warmth and affection. Bev's admiration for people such as his producer, Danny Davis (of Nashville Brass fame); for his arranger-director Bill Walker who took a bow every week on the Johnny Cash TV show; for the former Anita Kerr quartet (now the Nashville Sounds) who gave him vocal backing; for the eighteen-piece orchestra; for the recording technicians — was only surpassed by their obvious admiration for him and his professionalism.

Professionalism is the right word. I watched this assembled team painstakingly rehearse until they felt they were ready to cut a selection. Then, I listened carefully to what my untrained ear thought was a perfect rendition — only to see the entire number repeated again and again until everyone was satisfied. The demands Bev makes on himself — the perfection upon which he insists — was particularly revealing. No wonder he has been nominated for a "Grammy" award (the recording industry's equivalent of an Oscar) every year since 1963. (He won in 1966 with an album entitled *Southland Favorites.)*

I particularly enjoyed a fast-moving arrangement of "Do, Lord," a song I remember singing as a boy at a church camp, near St. Mary's, Ohio:

> **I've got a home in glory land that outshines the sun,**
> **I've got a home in glory land that outshines the sun,**
> **I've got a home in glory land that outshines the sun,**
> **Way beyond the blue.**
>
> **Do, Lord, oh do, Lord, oh do remember me,**
> **Do, Lord, oh do, Lord, oh do remember me,**
> **Do, Lord, oh do, Lord, oh do remember me,**
> **Way beyond the blue.**

What fun the band, the group and Bev all had tapping their feet and clapping hands as they sang this happy tune!

Balancing this rouser was the beautiful title selection for the album, the Judy Collins-revived revival classic, *Amazing Grace.* Introducing it, Bev recalled briefly at the outset the time he visited the grave of John Newton, its composer, in an Olney, England, churchyard, a short distance from the pulpit Newton once filled. Bev quoted the words inscribed on that headstone:

JOHN NEWTON, CLERK, ONCE AN INFIDEL AND LIBERTINE, A SERVANT OF SLAVES IN AFRICA, WAS BY THE RICH MERCY OF OUR LORD AND SAVIOUR JESUS CHRIST PRESERVED, RESTORED, PARDONED, AND APPOINTED TO PREACH THE FAITH HE HAD LONG LABORED TO DESTROY.

Then, he sang that old hymn:

> **Amazing grace! how sweet the sound,**
> **That saved a wretch like me!**
> **I once was lost, but now am found,**
> **Was blind, but now I see.**
>
> **'Twas grace that taught my heart to fear,**
> **And grace my fears relieved;**
> **How precious did that grace appear**
> **The hour I first believed!**

> Through many dangers, toils and snares,
>   I have already come;
> 'Tis grace hath brought me safe thus far,
>   And grace will lead me home.
>
> When we've been there ten thousand years,
>   Bright shining as the sun,
> We've no less days to sing God's praise
>   Than when we first begun.

When he had finished, the engineer's room outside the studio was nearly full of visitors and employees who had filed in to hear in detail the haunting lyrics and music that had filtered magnetically through the halls and offices of that famous recording studio. Not a few in the audience were watery-eyed as they walked away.

That's the moving effect Bev Shea has on people everywhere when he sings sacred music. Billy Graham has observed, "More than any other singer in modern times, Bev literally sings the message of Jesus Christ to the hearts of people."

In this book, George Beverly Shea talks about the music he loves, naming his favorite gospel songs and telling many warm, personal anecdotes about them that reveal why they mean so much to him. After reading the pages that follow I think you'll have an even greater appreciation for the man and his music.

FRED BAUER

Introduction

What makes a good hymn? A lasting hymn? One that catches on and stands the test of time?

I have often asked myself these questions as I select music for a Crusade, for a concert, for a record album, and I've never been able to see clearly why one song gains favor and another with apparently equal technical quality passes quickly from the scene. Others who are much more knowledgeable on the subject of sacred music than I have confessed equal bafflement. My conclusion is that gospel hymns which gain a kind of immortality have some special heart-touching quality, a spiritual depth and sincerity that surpasses others. Often they are rather simple melodies with simple messages and rather obvious end rhymes, but they touch people where they live; they move them, change them, inspire them.

Sometimes I find clues in the story behind a gospel hymn (not, however, that every "classic" in this special musical category has some dramatic story related to its writing). To the contrary, the lyrics for a good many of your favorites and mine were written by people who "just wrote poetry every day." And the melodies were composed by skilled craftsmen in this trade. But it must be added that many hymns do have a fascinating origin, like *Amazing Grace,* of which Fred Bauer has already spoken. It helps me to interpret the words when I know that John Newton, the author, was the son of a sea captain, who, after his mother's death, joined his father at age eleven on his ship.

I'm interested to know that he and his father apparently had a generation gap and they came to a parting of the ways, and that John's life turned into one of degradation — fighting, drinking, jail. Serving on a slave ship, he so infuriated the captain that he was made a slave of the slaves — another chapter in the Prodigal Son story. But then, somehow, John Newton came upon a copy of Thomas à Kempis' book, *Imitation of Christ,* and his heart responded. I can see him pondering those all-surrendering prayers of the author:

> O Lord, Thou knowest what is best for us; let this or that be done, as Thou shalt please. Give what Thou wilt, and how much Thou wilt, and when Thou wilt. Deal with me as Thou thinkest good, and as best pleaseth Thee. Set me where Thou wilt, and deal with me in all things as Thou wilt. Behold, I am Thy servant, prepared for all things; for I desire not to live unto myself, but unto Thee; and oh that I could do it worthily and perfectly!

But it took a storm at sea in which Newton almost lost his life for him to turn everything over to God. He became a minister at age thirty-nine and during his fifteen-year pastorate at Olney, England, he wrote the words to many hymns. The great composer William Cowper, also of Olney, set many of them to music and they collaborated on a famous hymnal. So with that background, I know what Newton is talking about when he writes about an amazing grace:

> **That saved a wretch like me!**
> **I once was lost, but now am found,**
> **Was blind, but now I see.**

I noted a few years ago that when *Christian Herald* magazine polled its readers, "Amazing Grace" was ninth on their all-time favorite list. A look at the results of that tally conducted by *Christian Herald* is most revealing:

THE FAVORITE FIFTY

1 The Old Rugged Cross
2 What A Friend We Have in Jesus
3 In the Garden
4 How Great Thou Art!
5 Sweet Hour of Prayer
6 Abide With Me
7 Rock of Ages
8 Nearer, My God, to Thee
9 Amazing Grace
10 Jesus, Lover of My Soul
11 Beyond the Sunset
12 Blessed Assurance
13 Lead, Kindly Light
14 My Faith Looks Up to Thee
15 Jesus, Savior, Pilot Me
16 Faith of Our Fathers
17 I Need Thee Every Hour
18 Have Thine Own Way
19 God Will Take Care of You
20 I Love to Tell the Story
21 Just As I Am
22 A Mighty Fortress
23 How Firm a Foundation
24 Ivory Palaces
25 Take Time to Be Holy
26 Holy, Holy, Holy
27 Whispering Hope

Like favorite Scripture verses, favorite songs have a way of under-girding us when "the way grows drear." Not long ago, I read a fascinating account of the *Pueblo* crew (*My Anchor Held* by Stephen Harris), captured by the North Koreans and imprisoned for eleven months. I read with great excitement the section which told about the men compiling a "Bible" from memory. Various ones contributed remembered verses and copied them onto the scraps of paper available. Then, at great personal risk, they passed them among each other, drawing strength and courage from the Word of God.

The author of that book wrote, "I prayed for strength not to hate the *Korcoms* (the Korean Communists). Scripture helped me. Fortunately, the chaplain friend who had shown me the way to Christ had recommended that I enroll in the Navigators' program of Scripture memory."

After reading that statement, I wondered what verses would sustain me if the freedom I take for granted living in the United States were ever withdrawn. What passages would help me uphold my faith? Surely, I would include:

● The Lord is my shepherd; I shall not want.
   He maketh me to lie down in green pastures: he leadeth me beside
      the still waters.
   He restoreth my soul: he leadeth me in the paths of righteousness for
      his name's sake.
   Yea, though I walk through the valley of the shadow of death, I will
      fear no evil: for thou art with me; thy rod and thy staff they
      comfort me.

Thou preparest a table before me in the presence of mine enemies:
   thou anointest my head with oil; my cup runneth over.
Surely goodness and mercy shall follow me all the days of my life:
   and I will dwell in the house of the Lord for ever. (Psalm 23)

- For God so loved the world that he gave his only begotten Son, that
  whosoever believeth in him should not perish, but have
  everlasting life. (John 3:16)

- In my Father's house are many mansions: if it were not so, I would
  have told you. I go to prepare a place for you. (John 14:2)

- Take therefore no thought for the morrow ... (Matthew 6:34)
  Consider the lilies of the field, how they grow; they toil not,
  neither do they spin: And yet I say unto you, That even Solomon
  in all his glory was not arrayed like one of these. (vs. 28,29)

And I'd have the verse that I use whenever someone asks me to sign
my John Henry for them, the twenty-eighth chapter of Psalms, verse
seven:

- The Lord is my strength and my shield; my heart trusted in him, and
  I am helped: therefore my heart greatly rejoiceth; and with my
  song will I praise him.

Yes, with my song I would praise Him. If I were denied my
freedom and access to my Bible, I, like the *Pueblo* crew, would have
to call on my memory and recite long-treasured verses, many of
which I learned as a boy. But after I had exhausted that source, I'm
sure I would turn to gospel music, the hymns. Which hymns? The
ones which have touched my heart, inspired me, sustained me. My
mail, hymn requests, and personal comments from Christian friends
indicate that many of the songs I've included in this book are your
favorites, too. I hope so.

To Him be the glory!

1

Songs I Grew Up On

My father, the Reverend A. J. Shea, and I were on an afternoon shopping trip for Mother, as I recall. When we came out of a store in Houghton, New York, where we had recently moved from Winchester, Ontario, we met a tall, elderly woman making her way slowly up the street. She was walking in that slow, mincing step older people sometimes do, cautious not to lose balance.

Dad tipped his hat and said good-day to her as we passed. She stopped and looked up to see who was speaking. Smiling sweetly, she returned his greeting.

"Do you know who that was, Son?" he asked me on up the way. I turned and watched as she continued her careful progress. Though a distinguished woman (whom I would now describe as looking a lot like Whistler's Mother) I had no idea who she was.

"That," said Dad, "was Mrs. Clara Tear Williams. She writes hymns." There was a near reverence in his voice, and though I was only eight years old, I was duly impressed. Already I was fascinated by music and anyone who was involved in it. Mother played the piano; Dad, the violin; and I was beginning to pick things out on the piano. I sometimes had trouble sitting through sermons on Sunday, or when we had evangelistic services nightly for extended periods, but I was never restless when it was time for the congregation to sing or when the choir or a soloist would present a special number. I liked the music part of a service best of all. Mother's carrot-on-the-stick was, "Be good now, Beverly, it won't be long before we'll sing."

When Dad and I got home that afternoon, I told Mother about meeting Mrs. Williams, the hymn writer. She smiled knowingly and nodded her head. Then she went to the piano bench and found a hymnal that contained one of Clara Tear Williams' compositions.

She explained that Mrs. Williams — a Weslyan Methodist like us — had written the words, but that the music had been written by

Ralph E. Hudson, an Ohio publisher who also was an evangelistic singer.

Placing the book on the music rack and sitting down to the piano, Mother began playing that song with me on the bench beside her. It was beautiful. Up until then, I guess I figured all the songs we sang in church were written and published by people who lived in far off places like New York. I couldn't get over the fact that we had a real live composer in our very own town.

A few years later, when I was in my teens and began to sing solos, I memorized the hymn that Mother played that day and sang it. It was entitled "Satisfied" or "All My Life Long." Maybe you've sung it:

> **All my life long I had panted**
> **For a drink from some cool spring,**
> **That I hoped would quench the burning**
> **Of the thirst I felt within.**
>
> **Feeding on the husks around me**
> **Till my strength was almost gone,**
> **Longed my soul for something better,**
> **Only still to hunger on.**
>
> **Poor was I and sought for riches,**
> **Something that would satisfy**
> **But the dust that gathered round me**
> **Only mocked my soul's sad cry.**
>
> **Hallelujah! I have found Him —**
> **Whom my soul so long has craved!**
> **Jesus satisfies my longings;**
> **Through His blood I now am saved.**

As I think back to that incident concerning Clara Tear Williams, I realize that from my earliest days I was encircled by music and by people who loved it. The gospel songs were ever being sung in our home.

My mother was the one who first brought music into my life. I suppose like many mothers she sang to me in the crib, repeating little nursery rhymes and children's Bible songs of the "Jesus Loves Me" variety, but the first song that really made an impression on me was Mother's wake-up theme song, her alarm clock tune, William Kirkpatrick's "Singing I Go." Every weekday morning she would wake the family by going to the piano, making a run down the keyboard, and then filling the house with her sweet soprano voice:

> Singing I go along life's road,
> Praising the Lord, praising the Lord,
> Singing I go along life's road,
> For Jesus has lifted my load.

It's a little painful as I write this to think I won't be hearing Mother sing it again. Last summer I received word that she was ill and I rushed to the hospital in Syracuse to see her. She'd undergone emergency surgery and despite her ninety years had weathered it well. However, complications arose, and it seemed to be God's will to take her home. With all of her children gathered around her (with the exception of Alton, a missionary in Africa) she passed away on September 1, 1971.

A number which has always had a warm spot in my heart because of its buoyant melody and positive, uplifting lyrics, it has been good to me over the years.

When I went to Chicago to work as an announcer for WMBI, the Moody Bible Institute radio station, I had a fifteen-minute program in the morning called "Hymns from the Chapel" and "Singing I Go" was my theme song. I got into the habit of taking the last note, "for Jesus has lifted my load" all the way down to E flat, slow *porto mento*. It drew quite a little attention, and I remember one woman writing to tell me that her children listened every morning to hear that low note, so I kept doing it.

Later I recorded the song for RCA and named an album after it, and I include it often when I sing sacred music concerts around the country. It serves as a good change of pace for more somber hymns. At these evening concerts, artists such as Tedd Smith, Don Hustad, or John Innes usually accompany me and also present some piano and/or organ selections.

One time in 1945, I remember Don and I were traveling with Bob Pierce doing a series of programs between Los Angeles and Seattle. At every concert along the way, I sang "Singing I Go." In each instance, I told the story of how Mother sang it each morning, and that it was she who taught it to me. Don Hustad heard the anecdote so many times, he knew my lines by heart. But at the end of the tour, I surprised him. After concluding on that low E flat at a program in Seattle, I turned to Don and said into the microphone, "But you know, Don, I don't recall that Mother taught me that note." He nearly fell off the piano bench, convulsed with laughter.

There is another incident I remember about that West Coast trip, too.

We often traveled by Greyhound bus, sometimes riding all night to our next stop, like the trip between Portland and Klamath Falls. Bob and Don didn't have any trouble sleeping that night I recall, but I did. Going over those mountains and around those sharp curves, I'd close my eyes for brief catnaps, but the fear that our driver would do the same kept me awake most of the time. When we arrived in the morning, I was so tired and wrinkled and hungry that all I could think about was a good meal, a shower, and some shut-eye, but the bright-eyed man who met us at the station had other plans.

"Boy, I was worried you wouldn't make it," he said, relieved. "We've arranged for you to sing on a radio program this morning and you're on the air in fifteen minutes."

Another early recollection of mine related to music happened when I was five years old. We were living in the Gladstone Street parsonage in Winchester, Ontario, at the time and our church, the Wesleyan Methodist, which Dad served for twenty years, was in the midst of evangelistic services.

One Saturday morning, about 10 A.M. the Reverend John Vennard, who was conducting the services, stopped by to discuss the music he intended to use in the next service.

Sitting down to our old Bell piano (a red mahogany instrument which had come from England about the time Mother and Dad were married, January 1, 1900, and has been in the family ever since), Mr. Vennard said, "Here are two new hymns that I like. They are both written by George Bennard, a minister who lives in Michigan. This one was just published last year (1913)." Then, he began to play and sing a hymn that was soon to sweep the world. Enraptured, I stood at the end of the piano and listened.

> **On a hill far away stood an old rugged cross,**
> **The emblem of suffering and shame;**
> **And I love that old cross where the dearest and best**
> **For a world of lost sinners was slain.**
>
> **So I'll cherish the old rugged cross**
> **Till my trophies at last I lay down;**
> **I will cling to the old rugged cross,**
> **And exchange it some day for a crown.**

After that he played and sang "Speak, My Lord," another beautiful hymn that was to receive great universal appreciation. I wonder how many times I have sung it since.

> **Speak, my Lord, speak, my Lord,**
> **Speak and I'll be quick to answer Thee,**
> **Speak, my Lord, speak, my Lord,**
> **Speak and I will answer, answer Thee.**

I first met the composer of those two great hymns in the early 1940s at Winona Lake, Indiana, 110 miles from Chicago. I'd go there to do remote broadcasts for WMBI, and during the summers Mr. Bennard was often on hand. Though a preacher — and a good one — he would sometimes sing. His voice was not trained or out of the ordinary but he had great feeling and expression and could really put over any hymn. I remember how moved I was when for the first time I heard him sing his own "The Old Rugged Cross."

Like my awe at seeing a real live composer as a boy when Dad pointed out Clara Tear Williams, I remember how people would whisper to each other whenever they saw Mr. Bennard on the Winona Lake grounds, at the sweet shop, or in the restaurant.

"He wrote the words to the 'Old Rugged Cross,'" mothers and fathers were telling their children. What a distinguished looking man — slight of build, short, with glasses, the most memorable thing about him was his long, white hair. He was ahead of his time!

In the summer, my wife Erma and I often drive through his home-town, Albion, Michigan, on our way to our cabin in Quebec.

I never drive through there but what I am tempted to look up the Chamber of Commerce and upbraid them for not identifying Albion on their city limits signs as THE HOME OF GEORGE BENNARD, COMPOSER OF AMERICA'S FAVORITE HYMN, "THE OLD RUGGED CROSS." One of these days I'll get up my nerve and make that suggestion.

Speaking of Winona Lake and George Bennard, one cannot go on without mentioning Homer Rodeheaver who, more than anyone else, popularized "The Old Rugged Cross." Traveling around the country with Billy Sunday, Mr. Rodeheaver's rendition of it was par excellence. Of course, his music publishing company was nearby so I seldom came to Winona Lake without seeing and talking with him. Like George Bennard, Mr. Rodeheaver was not tall, but he was more stocky than Mr. Bennard. Both had one thing in common: huge smiles. They seemed eternally happy to me.

I also heard Mr. Rodeheaver sing often in those days. One of my favorites by him was "Then Jesus Came." He wrote the music to those tender Oswald J. Smith lyrics.

One sat alone beside the highway begging,
His eyes were blind, the light he could not see;
He clutched his rags and shivered in the shadows,
Then Jesus came and bade his darkness flee.

When Jesus comes the tempter's power is broken;
When Jesus comes the tears are wiped away.
He takes the gloom and fills the life with glory.
For all is changed when Jesus comes to stay.

Not only did Homer Rodeheaver do great justice to that song with his rich baritone voice, he added much meaning by acting out certain portions as he sang: "One sat alone" ... "blinded and could not see" ... "clutched his rags" ... "tears are wiped away...."

When I heard him, he also did part of the hymn in narration — a dramatic, memorable rendition.

It was a great thrill to meet Mr. Rodeheaver in person. The first time I can recall hearing him was on a record when I was fourteen and living in Ottawa, Canada. Across the street from our Metcalf Street parsonage, I heard this beautiful duet singing "Sunrise." It was coming from the front porch of the Beardsleys. (Mr. Beardsley owned a shoe store in Ottawa.)

I ran over to hear the end of it, and asked if they would play it again. Winding up the mahogany Victrola — something of a show piece at that time — Mr. Beardsley set the needle back at the beginning, and I listened to Homer Rodeheaver and a Mrs. Asher combine their beautiful voices:

When I shall come to the end of my way,
When I shall rest at the close of life's day,
When "Welcome home" I shall hear Jesus say,
O that will be sunrise for me!

There are so many people who come to mind when I think of those visits to Winona Lake. People such as Virgil and Blanche Brock, whose singing and hymn writing has blessed millions. They were often in attendance during summer meetings at the Billy Sunday pavilion.

It was beautiful Winona Lake which helped inspire their most famous hymn, "Beyond the Sunset." The Brocks were prolific composers whose writing reportedly came most often on inspiration. A phrase from a sermon, a fragment of conversation, a reading from Scripture, some beautiful sight from nature, might set this great husband and wife team in the mood for writing, and they would interrupt whatever they were doing. More than once they reportedly awakened in the middle of the night and inspired by some thought, would write together until morning, Mrs. Brock the music, Mr. Brock the words.

"Beyond the Sunset" was penned in 1936, about the time I first started visiting the Indiana retreat center for WMBI. According to the oft-repeated story, the Brocks were guests of Mr. Rodeheaver, staying at his home on Rainbow Point. After dinner, the Brocks and other guests sat watching a breathtaking sunset across the lake. One of the guests, Horace Burr, a blind man, surprised the group when he said, "I've never seen a more beautiful sunset!"

"How can you say that?" Virgil Brock inquired.

"I see through the eyes of others," he answered. "I even see beyond the sunset."

The combination of the beautiful reflection of the sun across the lake and Mr. Burr's comment triggered Mr. Brock's mind. "Beyond the sunset," he repeated. "Beyond the sunset." The second time he began to hum a tune, improvising other words as he did. Blanche Brock heard him, quietly excused herself and walked into the house where on Mr. Rodeheaver's piano, she fleshed out the melody her husband had begun.

When Mrs. Brock died in 1958, she was buried in Warsaw, Indiana. There in that cemetery on her stone are carved the words and music to one of the world's all-time favorite songs, "Beyond the Sunset."

> **Beyond the sunset, O blissful morning,**
> **When with our Saviour heaven is begun.**
> **Earth's toiling ended, O glorious dawning,**
> **Beyond the sunset, when day is done.**

C. Austin Miles, composer of "In the Garden," B.D. Ackley, composer of many loved hymns, and Mrs. Charles Cowman, who with her husband edited that famous devotional, *Streams in the Desert,* all come to mind when I think of my visits to Winona Lake.

Erma and I first met Mr. Ackley on our honeymoon. Married in 1934 in Ottawa, we made the traditional trip to Niagara Falls, New York, after the wedding. There, one day we visited the famous Churchill Tabernacle from which emanated the popular "Back Home Hour." The Reverend B. D. Ackley was the pianist on the program. An Englishman, who had found the Lord in an American Keswick meeting in New Jersey, he went on to write and play for Homer Rodeheaver. Mr. Ackley's great music will inspire men for many years to come.

Recently, I had opportunity to talk with Mrs. Herbert Dye, Mr. Ackley's daughter, who now makes her home at Winona Lake. Reminiscing about the musical work of her father and uncle, Mrs. Dye called to mind many Ackley-written hymns including "Amazed" and one that was featured often by Dr. Charles Fuller on his "Old Fashioned Revival Hour" — "When I Kneel Down to Pray."

Mrs. Cowman's presence at Winona Lake brings to mind an excerpt from *Streams in the Desert* which I memorized when I was living in Jersey City, outside New York. One day Mother handed me the book with a passage marked. "Maybe you'd like to commit this to memory," she said. "It's a beautiful thought."

I agreed and did memorize it, and can still recite it:

Get up early, go to the mountains and watch God make a morning. The dull gray will give way as God pushes the sun toward the horizon and there will be tints and hues of every shade as the full orbed sun bursts into view. And as the king of the day moves forward majestically flooding the earth and every lowly vale, listen to the music of heaven's choir as it sings of the majesty of God and the glory of the morning. In the hush of the earthly dawn, I hear a voice saying, "I am with you all the day. Rejoice! Rejoice!"

One of my pet peeves is that many of our schools don't encourage more memory work. I think it is a good discipline, and furthermore, it can be a great joy in later years to recall some meaningful poem, a verse of song, Scripture, or quote from great literature. I recommend learning some things by heart!

Before I wandered off (I'll be doing that often in this book), and got to talking about "The Old Rugged Cross," George Bennard and my first meeting of him at Winona Lake, I was reminiscing about my childhood music experiences. As I told you, Mother's great love of music was infectious and she, more than anyone else, is responsible for stirring my interest, fanning the coals inside me, and encouraging me to try. Thinking back to those days when she taught me the chords and worked with me at the piano, I realize how important a role parents play in pointing children, unearthing some God-given talent and giving a child confidence in that area. A big kid, awkward, unsure, timid, shy, I needed some field in which I felt comfortable, and music proved to be that field. It is hard for me to imagine — now — that I would have gone any other direction, but in retrospect I see clearly that Mother was the impetus behind my gravitation to music as a life's work.

When I was about eight, I contracted a mysterious throat infection which kept me out of school much of the third and fourth grades. Infected tonsils seemed to be the root of the problem and they were removed, but apparently the poison from them had spread throughout my whole system and the aftereffects lingered for months and months. Today, I suppose penicillin would clear up such a problem in a matter of days. Then, I was put to bed and told to rest.

Mother became my schoolteacher and the kitchen my classroom. While she would cook and bake, I'd sit at the table reading or reciting. She would come over occasionally to give me some help when I got stuck on a word or arithmetic problem. Mother thought one could learn to read as well from the Bible as any other book so I was often given this Book to use. I also read poems (usually of a spiritual nature); and, upon occasion, she would ask me to read the verses from a hymnal. Sometimes, moved by a particular hymn, Mother would take me into the living room, where our Bell piano sat, and play and sing the song to me. Then she would ask me to try it. Though I was no child prodigy, I could hack my way through a song at a fairly early age and because of her coaching and compliments, I kept practicing — and improving.

My sisters Pauline and Mary also played the piano. Encouraged by Dad, the whole family was often gathered around the keyboard. The Bell piano was second only to the kitchen table as a family gathering place.

My mother was not surprised by my early interest in music, though. She had taken to it at a young age herself, prompted by God-fearing, music-loving parents. The fact that she composed a hymn herself in her teens is evidence of her seriousness. The number was called "Adoration." I recorded it in an album called *More Songs of the Southland* and it is full of meaning and beauty.

I was exposed to music on every hand. In addition to singing and chording at the piano, I also put in a stint on the violin. The fact that my parents put out thirteen dollars for a violin for me from their very limited finances is convincing evidence that music had a high standing on their list of priorities!

Dad liked the violin, and could play it quite well, I discovered. Only his repertoire was limited to square-dance music which he played as a young man. By this time, though, those Saturday night hoedowns were a thing of the past. One of Dad's violin favorites which I can remember him playing was "Turkey in the Straw." Somehow it was out of character for him, however, and after a few bars, he would laugh and hand the instrument back to me.

I wasn't very good on "Turkey in the Straw," but I did learn "Somewhere a Voice Is Calling" and "Absent" which I used to entertain a beautiful, young gal named Erma Scharfe. Eventually, she agreed to marry me and she has been putting up with me for nearly thirty-six years now. That may be because I put up the violin! I do have that old violin in my possession again. My brother Alton found it in his attic not long ago and gave it to me.

The first time I played the violin in public came at a month-long camp meeting in Westport, Ontario. I'd gone there with Fred and Kitty Suffield, evangelist friends of my parents who had invited me to go along and help them. As I was about seventeen, I imagine I was invited more out of the kindness of their hearts than for the contribution I might make.

What a great team they were! Fred always said that Kitty was sent to him by a Providential snowstorm. He explained by telling how he was awakened by a pounding at his farmhouse door one stormy winter night. When he answered the door, a near-freezing man told him that he was a passenger from a train that had become marooned in the heavy snow. Others on the train were in danger of freezing. Fred dressed hurriedly, lit a lantern and followed the man across snow-covered fields to the stranded passengers. There, he invited them to take shelter at his farm, and many went with him to safety. One of his grateful guests that night was Kitty, who later wrote to thank him for his kindness. A correspondence followed and eventually they fell in love and married.

At a Westport meeting, as I related in *Then Sings My Soul,* I made my first attempt as a vocal soloist. To the accompaniment of Kitty, I sang "He Died of a Broken Heart" — or tried to sing it! I cracked on one of the high notes, but Kitty just kept smiling and played on. I was embarrassed to tears, but when I suggested that I better not try any more solos, she would not hear of it. The next time I sang it in a lower key, and I didn't crack. Still, I never hear those words but what I don't wince. Learning to sing, developing the confidence to hit the high notes and the low ones takes much practice, I learned — painfully. No wonder I remember my first solo.

> **He died of a broken heart — for me,**
> **He died of a broken heart,**
> **O wonderous thought how can it be,**
> **He died of a broken heart.**

Though Fred Suffield has gone home to be with the Lord he preached so effectively about, Kitty is still living — in Los Angeles. I try to see her or give her a call whenever I'm in the area. She wrote many gospel songs that I like, including "Little Is Much."

In the harvest fields now ripened
There's a work for all to do,
Hark! The voice of God is calling,
"To the harvest," calling you.

Little is much when God is in it,
Labor not for wealth or fame
There's a crown and you can win it
When you go in Jesus' name.

Does the place we're called to labor
Seem so small and little known?
It is great when God is in it
And He'll not forget His own.

But her most famous composition (written with her husband) and one that is a particular favorite of mine is "God Is Still on the Throne."

God is still on the throne
And He will remember His own,
Though trials may press us
And burdens distress us
He never will leave us alone....

Back in Ottawa after that confidence-building summer with Fred and Kitty, I began to sing more in public. I joined up with three other students who loved to sing and we formed a quartet. One of the guys, our first tenor, was Alonzo Scharfe and it was through his friendship that I met his sister, Erma.

I'll never forget that they put us on the program the day the prestigious Christian and Missionary Alliance Church was dedicated. Before 2,500 people including the mayor, we sang "Come Over Into the Land of Corn and Wine."

Come over, come over
To the land of corn and wine,
There's nothing to compare
With the hidden treasures there....

When we got to the last chorus, we were going so fast we nearly ran right through the land of corn and wine, but by some miracle we finished together. Maybe it was answered prayer. I know Mother and Dad were present that day, and I'm sure Mother began praying when our quartet started speeding. Anyway, we tried and did well enough that our spirit was not broken.

When I think back to the kindness of people who tolerated my early fumblings, I realize how important it is for adults to temper criticism with understanding and patience — otherwise, I would have been washed out of the musical field at an early age.

Churches who find places for young pianists and soloists in their services are to be commended. I know it is a temptation to work with older, more accomplished musicians, but encouraging young people and giving them an opportunity to develop their God-given talents is most important. Not long ago, I heard some young people sing a modern folk-hymn in church to the accompaniment of a guitar. Not only were the lyrics moving, but the guitar was a beautiful addition. New forms of music should not be excluded from church, especially when they are meaningful to young people.

Some of the music I hear today sounds strange to my ears, but I try to keep an open mind to all varieties, realizing that too often we reject the unfamiliar without a fair trial. It's human nature to say we don't like what we don't know, but it's wisdom and a sign of eternal youth to give new things a chance.

On the subjects of young people and gospel music, I might interject right here what to me are the most important qualifications for people involved with music of a spiritual bent. I receive letters regularly from young people asking for career advice.

> I'd like to become a singer of gospel hymns as my lifework; how do I proceed?

> I like to write religious poetry, and think I'd like to write lyrics for hymns; how do I go about it?

> I play the piano and plan to study it in college. Is there a place in the sacred music field for a professional pianist?

Though most of the inquiries I receive are very subjective — matters which will take time and application and prayer to resolve — there are some basic considerations. One of these has to do with degree of involvement. To become a minister of the Gospel, one needs to attend a seminary and prepare himself for his calling.

To become a Christian worker, one needs to study the Bible and have some understanding of Scripture before he can talk to someone else about his faith, but his degree of training will seldom be as intensive as an ordained minister's.

Much the same is true of the gospel music field. People on the Billy Graham musical team such as Cliff Barrows, Tedd Smith and John Innes have prepared themselves professionally for their ministries. People who direct local church choirs or sing in them, organists or pianists may or may not have college degrees in music, but they are students of the hymns and continue to grow in their abilities by practicing. The point I'm trying to make is, that there are many ways of serving God through music, but whether professional or part-time, all callings make certain demands. There are at least four qualifications that I think essential:

First, to sing the words of the hymns with conviction, one needs to believe that they are true. Whole-heartedness is essential. Without belief, the power of the lyrics fades. It's not hard to tell from listening to someone sing whether or not he or she is attuned with the words of a song.

Second, a mechanical one: you must have the ability to carry a tune if you're going to be an effective music witness. If you have no sense of melody, your area of service no doubt lies in another direction, but most of us have been given about the same physical equipment. The difference is in the development of it, which brings me to:

Third, you must be willing to work, listen, be taught, practice and apply yourself if you are going to improve. This is true in any discipline and music is no exception. I figure I have been "going to school" for better than forty years, and every day I learn something new from the people with whom I come in contact. Don Hustad, who is now a professor at the Southern Baptist Seminary in Louisville, is a good example. Though he is one of the most knowledgeable people that I know in the field of sacred music, he never has stopped learning.

A person who wants to be a part of this field must love music very much.

Fourth (and maybe most important), gospel music needs people who want to give themselves to a cause, namely the work of Jesus Christ. There is no room for peacocks who make attention-getting shrieks or grand displays of their beautiful feathers. Working in the religious music field is not *show business,* but *God business,* and unless you can subordinate your own ego, it's probably best you use your talent in another way. That saying which I've seen on so many pulpits — one that faces the singer or speaker — is apropos: WE WOULD SEE JESUS.

I remember the first time I played the organ in public. It was at the Fifth Avenue Church in Ottawa. Though it was a small reed organ, it really captivated me. It had more tonal range than any reed organ I'd ever played. I particularly liked the celeste stop which cancelled the lefthand bass. One of my chums, Asa MacIntosh, managed to get permission for me to play it occasionally and he would listen appreciatively while I practiced.

It was a beautiful Estey reed organ that produced some heavenly *vox humana* sounds. When I played "Safe in the Arms of Jesus," Asa called up from where he was sitting, "Boy, Bev, that is really terrific. You sound great."

Lest anyone think Asa and I spent all our time in church, however, let me dispel that notion by telling you how we occasionally passed time after supper.

Hiding in the bushes along Bank Street, we would plant an empty wallet on the sidewalk and attach fishing tackle to it. Then we'd wait in the bushes until somebody would come along and spot the billfold. When he or she would bend down to pick it up, we'd give the line a jerk and reel it in. That was our idea of devilment.

How shaken I was when Asa became ill at age fifteen, suffering from some heart malfunction. Within a few weeks he wasted away from what appeared to be fine health to death.

When word came that he had died, his mother asked me if I would play the organ at his funeral. "Asa told me how beautifully you play 'Safe in the Arms of Jesus.' Would you do that hymn for us?"

I agreed. At age fifteen, I drew one of the toughest assignments I've ever had, but I'm sure that hymn was a comfort to Asa's family as it has been to so many at times of bereavement. The words offer wonderful reassurance:

> Safe in the arms of Jesus,
> Safe on His gentle breast
> There by His love o'ershadowed,
> Sweetly my soul shall rest.

I have never forgotten that Ottawa organ. "Some day I'm going to own one of my own," I told Erma when we were still dating. Well, many, many years later while I was reading the *Chicago Tribune* one morning I saw an ad for reed organs. I followed it up, and went to the home of an old man on Chicago's North Side. There in his basement were dozens of old organs including an Estey just like the one I played in Asa's church. It was the exact same model — made in about 1915 I'd guess — about four feet high and five feet wide.

Pressing the keys and hitting a chord, I could tell it was in excellent condition. Then, I noticed that celeste stop which created that haunting sound of muted strings. I anxiously pulled the stop and began to play "Safe in the Arms of Jesus." There it was, that magnificent tone. I completely forgot myself and played and sang a whole verse of that hymn.

Then, I heard the man shuffle his feet before self-consciously asking, "You like it?"

"Yes, I do."

"Well, she's yours for sixty-five dollars." I would have paid him much more.

Today, it occupies a corner of our basement. I have stripped all the panels from it, have removed the varnish and am refinishing it. Erma says I can bring it upstairs into our recreation room when I complete the job — which will be some time around 1985 at my present pace.

Meanwhile, I content myself with a few chords every time I go to the basement on some mundane chore quite incongruous with the ethereal sounds which come from my prized Estey.

In 1967, I recorded "Safe in the Arms of Jesus" for RCA. I included it in an album called *Be Still My Soul.*

After the album was finished but before it was released, I flew to New York to attend a testimonial luncheon arranged by The National Association of Recording Arts and Sciences to honor Steve Sholes, an RCA vice-president who was my first A & R (Artist and Repertoire) man. He worked with such superstars as Eddy Arnold, Chet Atkins, and Elvis Presley. The next day following the luncheon, I went to Steve's office to hear my soon-to-be-released album. After Steve and I had heard "Safe in the Arms of Jesus," he told me how much the words meant to him.

It was not an offhand comment. He had come forward to make a public confession during our Pittsburgh Crusade. His decision, his comment about "Safe in the Arms of Jesus" and all his kindnesses to me returned to mind a few weeks later when I received word in Australia that Steve Sholes, one of the most beloved men in the recording industry, had died of a heart attack in Nashville.

As most of you know, "Safe in the Arms of Jesus," is a William H. Doane-Fanny Crosby hymn. It was written in 1869 in New York City. Reportedly, Mr. Doane brought the music to Mrs. Crosby and asked her to write words for it.

"Let me hear it," she said. The blind woman sat attentively listening while he played his composition on a small organ. When he had finished Mrs. Crosby told him:

"That says we are safe in the arms of Jesus. Let me see what I can do with it." Half an hour later, she was back with the lyrics as we know them more than a hundred years later.

Incidentally, in that same year, Mr. Doane gave Mrs. Crosby another tune which was to gain great favor in gospel hymn circles. To that music she set the words to "Jesus, Keep Me Near the Cross."

> **In the cross, in the cross**
> **Be my glory ever,**
> **Till my raptured soul shall find**
> **Rest beyond the river.**

Speaking of Steve Sholes' decision at Pittsburgh brings to mind my own commitment to Christ. All my brothers and sisters had turned their lives over to the Lord except me. Though I was a believer, I had not made a public statement to that effect — and when I still hadn't at age eighteen, I suppose my family became a little concerned. I know why I hadn't gone forward: I was just too shy.

Then Kitty and Fred Suffield came to Dad's church in Ottawa for revival services. Dad was preaching when Fred found the Lord. He went into evangelistic work in part because of Dad's encouragement, so they were especially close friends. Each night I attended the service and each night at the altar call I would sing the songs of invitation fervently and passionately, but did not budge from my spot in the very last pew.

"Oh, Why Not Tonight," "I Am Praying for You," "Let the Saviour In," "Only Trust Him," "Pass Me Not," "Almost Persuaded" — I sang them all without surrendering. Finally, on the last night of special services, I went forward to the music that has served as background for millions of similar decisions.

> **Just as I am, without one plea,**
> **But that Thy blood was shed for me,**
> **And that Thou bidd'st me come to Thee,**
> **O Lamb of God, I come! I come!**
>
> **Just as I am, and waiting not**
> **To rid my soul of one dark blot,**
> **To Thee whose blood can cleanse each spot,**
> **O Lamb of God, I come! I come!**
>
> **Just as I am, though tossed about**
> **With many a conflict, many a doubt,**
> **Fightings and fears within, without,**
> **O Lamb of God, I come! I come!**

> **Just as I am, poor, wretched, blind;**
> **Sight, riches, healing of the mind,**
> **Yea, all I need, in Thee I find,**
> **O Lamb of God, I come! I come!**

> **Just as I am, Thou wilt receive,**
> **Wilt welcome, pardon, cleanse, relieve;**
> **Because Thy promise I believe,**
> **O Lamb of God, I come! I come!**

"Just As I Am" is probably the most famous invitational hymn of them all. We use it often in our Crusades because it says it all.

It has an interesting story behind its writing.

In 1836, lyricist Charlotte Elliott, a Londoner and a person of no little musical education, suffered a breakdown and became bedridden at age thirty-three. When a minister came to visit her he inquired if she were a Christian. The woman said in effect that that was a matter between her and God. But a few weeks later, she invited him back and in a more contrite spirit asked:

"How does one come to Christ?"

"Why, just come to Him as you are," the minister answered. And that is what she did. Fourteen years later, looking back on that turning point in her life, she wrote the words which were set to music by William Bradbury.

Someone asked me one day why only the choir sings the invitation hymn at Crusades. I had an answer.

One day I told Billy Graham about my conversion experience, noting that "I think I was actually finding release from the conviction I was under by singing good and loud. Instead of going forward, I *sang.*"

"That's very interesting, Bev," he said.

That night when the organist began playing the invitational hymn, I was pleasantly surprised to hear Billy say, "Now while the *choir* is singing 'Just As I Am'...."

2

Songs That Led to a Life's Work

"What do you think you'd like to do with your life, Son?" Dad asked me one day toward the end of my high-school years.

I told him I wasn't sure, but that I hoped to find the answer at Houghton College. I already had made plans to enroll there in a general course of study, and though I hoped to sing in the glee club as an extra-curricular activity, the thought of pursuing a career in music didn't enter my head. First of all, I had very little confidence in my voice or my ability to use it. Second, no one I knew was making a living singing or playing gospel hymns. No, I'd have to find some utilitarian job. I did hope to serve the Lord in some way, but in what way I wasn't sure. One thing of which I was certain: I would never be a minister.

I was so shy, so tongue-tied and such a mumbler when I stood to speak that no one ever suggested I might some day follow in Dad's footsteps, and I certainly never entertained the idea.

There followed a memorable year at Houghton College — a year only, because it was 1928-29 and there just wasn't enough money to continue. But it was another link in my training. Professor Herman Baker gave me some vocal help that has proved valuable. He always advised pupils that they should study their music until it became a part of their heart and soul.

It was another way of saying, "Anything worth doing is worth doing right," My Scriptural injunction for striving for perfection comes from 2 Timothy 2:15: *Study to shew thyself approved unto God, a workman that needeth not to be ashamed....*

One number I learned to love that year was "Remember Now Thy Creator" and though it was beyond my capabilities then I eventually learned it and have used it upon occasion. I love its thought, drawn from Ecclesiastes 11:9.

Rejoice, O young man, in thy youth; and let thy heart cheer thee in the days of thy youth, and walk in the ways of thine heart, and in the sight of thine eyes; but know thou that for all these things God will bring thee into judgment.

Family financial problems limited my college to one year, 1928-29. I decided to work a while and then return, but as they say, "One thing led to another," and it never happened.

Dad had accepted a call to a Jersey City church outside New York City so I went to join my family there. I soon had a job working in the medical department of Mutual of New York (MONY), the life insurance company. I went to work for them just two months before the stock market crash, and stayed there almost nine years.

Meanwhile, I kept busy with my singing and playing. Mother and I alternated Sundays at church, playing an old motorized reed organ. I spent hours each week preparing music to be in the service, the designated hymns, the invitation, the offertory. One of my favorite offertory numbers was:

> **Have Thine own way, Lord, have Thine own way!**
> **Thou art the Potter; I am the clay,**
> **Mould me and make me after Thy will,**
> **While I am waiting, yielded and still.**

The music for this great hymn was written in 1907 by George C. Stebbins, a wonderful Christian composer whom I got to meet a few years later.

That was in 1943. I helped Jack Wyrtzen with his evangelistic work that summer and one day he invited me to go with him to visit Mr. Stebbins, who at age ninety-five was retired and living with a relative in the Catskills. What a pleasure to meet him. Though hard-of-hearing, he was very alert and pleased to have visitors. A tall man with whiskers, he exuded great dignity and warmth. Jack introduced us and suggested I sing "There is a Green Hill Far Away," one of Mr. Stebbins's many musical contributions. (The words were written by Cecil F. Alexander) and while others have put this poem to music, Stebbins' version is the most requested.

"Get close to his ear, Bev," Jack coached and I did as I sang:

> **There is a green hill far away**
> **Without a city wall,**
> **Where my dear Lord was crucified**
> **Who died to save us all.**

> O dearly, dearly, has He loved
> And we must love Him, too,
> And trust in His redeeming blood
> And try His work to do.

When I had finished, Mr. Stebbins smiled and nodded his head.

"Wonderful. A fine job. Your voice reminds me of my friend Carlton Booth."

I thanked him for the compliment. Being compared to a fine singer like Carlton was high praise indeed. However, Jack had all he could do to keep from laughing out loud, and seeing him cover his face almost broke me up. The joke was that Carlton Booth is a high tenor and I'm a bass baritone or so they tell me. Mr. Stebbins' deafness aside, he meant well, and I accepted his comment as the compliment it was intended.

I will never forget the moving prayer he gave before Jack and I left. Taking our hands, he prayed:

"Dear Lord, we thank Thee for this visit from Thy servants. Thank You for gospel music, the inspiration it gives. And thank You for sending these people — Mr. Wyrtzen and Mr. Shea who love to tell others about You through sermons and song. Thank You for the music You placed on my heart and for letting me serve You through music. Bless these men, guide them and strengthen them as they carry on the work that others before them have begun. We give You the glory. In Jesus' Name, Amen."

That day Mr. Stebbins gave me an autographed copy of his book, *Reminiscences and Gospel Hymn Stories* which I cherish very much to this day. The pen shook so hard as he signed the book that he needed to steady it with his other hand, but I had to admire his marvelous spirit. Incidentally, the book, which was published in 1924, is a treasury of fascinating gospel hymn stories, dating from 1869 when Mr. Stebbins' talent and Christian dedication were first recognized by many well-known religious figures at that time. He wrote the melody for hundreds of hymns, some of which are still favorites. To Mr. Stebbins' credit are such tunes as "Saviour, Breathe An Evening Blessing" (or "Evening Prayer"), "Ye Must Be Born Again" (with W. T. Sleeper) and that wonderful, old invitational "Jesus, I Come," also written with Mr. Sleeper:

> Out of my bondage, sorrow and night,
> Jesus, I come, Jesus, I come,
> Into Thy freedom, gladness and light
> Jesus, I come to Thee.

> Out of my sickness into Thy health,
> Out of my want and into Thy wealth
> Out of my sin and into Thyself
> Jesus I come to Thee.

Mr. Stebbins also wrote the music for "True Hearted, Whole Hearted," "Take Time to Be Holy" and several of Aunt Fanny Crosby's poems such as "Jesus Is Tenderly Calling" and "Saved by Grace" — two hymns I haven't heard lately. They deserve remembering. Many a lost soul has made his way to an altar of prayer while singing:

> Jesus is tenderly calling thee home,
> Calling today, calling today;
> Why from the sunshine of love wilt thou roam,
> Farther and farther away?
>
> Calling today, calling today
> Jesus is calling, Is tenderly calling today.

And how many times have you sung these words?

> Some day the silver chord will break
> And I no more as now shall sing;
> But O, the joy when I shall wake
> Within the palace of the King!
>
> And I shall see Him face to face,
> And tell the story — Saved by grace;
> And I shall see Him face to face
> And tell the story — Saved by grace.

How exciting to read through Mr. Stebbins' memoirs as he recalls his travels and ministry with Dwight L. Moody, Major D. W. Whittle, Philip P. Bliss, Ira D. Sankey, William H. Doane, James McGranahan, William Kirkpatrick, Rev. George F. Pentecost, George Root, H. R. Palmer, and many other evangelical leaders of the day.

The book is full of insight into the personalities and characters of many Christians whose contributions to God's work are well known, but whose lives are not. For example, I read with interest a passage which told about Mr. Stebbins' last meeting with Philip P. Bliss, one of the giants of gospel hymn writing ("Almost Persuaded," "Wonderful Words of Life," "Hallelujah," "What a Saviour," "Let the Lower Lights Be Burning," "The Light of the World is Jesus"). Wrote Mr. Stebbins:

I was appointed (by D. L. Moody) to assist George C. Needham in his work in Oshkosh, Wisconsin, and later, with Charles Inglis of England, I was sent to one of the smaller churches of South Chicago. On entering the railway station on my way to this second appointment, I found Mr. and Mrs. Bliss waiting for the train I was to take.

While bidding goodbye to Mrs. Stebbins and our son, then a small boy, Mr. and Mrs. Bliss were reminded of their two boys in the home of friends in Rome, Pennsylvania, and tears came to their eyes.

After leaving Chicago, Mr. Bliss fell asleep, with his head resting on his wife's shoulder. He was still sleeping when my destination was reached. As I rose to pass out, I said to Mrs. Bliss, "Don't disturb him." She replied: "Oh, yes! He would be disappointed if he did not say goodbye." As he wakened and realized I was leaving, he followed me onto the platform with kindest wishes and parting words.

This proved to be the last time I saw him, for he and Mrs. Bliss at the conclusion of the meetings at Peoria, went to their children to spend the holidays, and on their way back to Chicago, a few days later, they met their tragic death at Ashtabula, Ohio.

Reminiscences and Gospel Hymn Stories

The death of Mr. and Mrs. Bliss on December 29, 1876, was indeed tragic. Mr. Bliss was just thirty-eight and at the time was producing some of his best hymns. A writer of words and music, and a soloist and song leader as well (he often conducted services with Major Whittle), Mr. Bliss is described as handsome, tall and with a strong, moving bass baritone voice. Yet, friends seemed to be more impressed with his gentleness than anything else. They mourned in great numbers when he and his wife lost their lives in a fiery train wreck. Reportedly, Mr. Bliss survived the crash and climbed through a broken window to safety, but then returned to the coach trying to rescue his wife. Neither got out. In Mr. Bliss' effects was found a copy of an unpublished hymn he had recently completed:

> **I will sing of my Redeemer**
> **And His wondrous love to me;**
> **On the cruel cross He suffered,**
> **From the curse to set me free.**

> **I will tell the wondrous story,**
> **How my lost estate to save,**
> **In His boundless love and mercy,**
> **He the ransom freely gave.**

I will praise my dear Redeemer,
  His triumphant power I'll tell,
How the victory He giveth
  Over sin, and death, and hell.

I will sing of my Redeemer
  And His heavenly love for me;
He from death to life hath brought me,
  Son of God, with Him to be.

Sing, oh, sing of my Redeemer,
  With His blood He purchased me,
On the cross He sealed my pardon,
  Paid the debt, and made me free.

I was telling you about those early days in New York City where I was working for an insurance company and living with Mother and Dad in Jersey City, playing the organ at the Wesleyan Church. It was that organ which was used to introduce the first hymn I ever wrote. Once again Mother — my musical guardian — had a part.

A lover of beauty be it a flower, a bird, a poem, an ennobling quotation — whatever — Mother was a collector. What she collected most, though, was friends. A person who gave herself without qualification to others, she won so many to her with her warmth, her wit, and her charm.

With friends and family she loved to share poetry and she always had some verse in hand copied from a book or clipped from a magazine. As I've told before, it was her practice of leaving such writing on the piano music rack which led to my writing "I'd Rather Have Jesus" when I was twenty. The same Sunday morning I read those wonderful words for the first time, I wrote music for them and used the song that same day in my father's church service. Of course, Mrs. Rhea F. Miller is the catalyst. Without her inspiring lyrics, there would have been no song. That's true with a number of our church classics. Without the faith and talented pen of such poets as Longfellow, Phillips Brooks, William Cullen Bryant, Oliver Wendell Holmes, Martin Luther, Henry Van Dyke, Charles Wesley, Isaac Watts, Thomas Moore, Rudyard Kipling, John Milton, Alfred Tennyson, William Wordsworth, and other famous writers, we would have been denied the joy of many a great hymn.

Over the years, I've not sung any song more than "I'd Rather Have Jesus," but I never tire of Mrs. Miller's heartfelt words.

All those years in New York, I studied voice and gained experience by singing in church choirs and on radio. Like so many things in life, all of these opportunities were jigsaw puzzle pieces that eventually fit into a pattern — though that pattern was very vague then.

One of the first men I studied under lived in the West Seventies. I can't remember his name which is just as well. Though well qualified, his goals and mine were far different, and we soon parted company.

For a few weeks, I rode the subway uptown to take lessons but in addition to not being *simpatico* to gospel music, this man nearly broke me — financially. For twenty minutes of instruction (and he practically set an alarm clock to make sure he didn't give me any extra time) he charged ten dollars. That was about a third of my salary then. My seriousness about music is reflected in the fact that I went to him at all.

I had better luck with his successors — the likes of Emerson Williams and Price Boone. I'll never forget my auditon with Emerson Williams, who sang bass on NBC with the famous Revelers Quartet. He was some kind of singer. What a voice! He asked me to do something I liked and I pulled the music to "The Love of God" out of my case. After I had sung it, he had tears in his eyes and some kind words for me. He agreed to take me on as a student, and I was pleased, though I had a feeling my selection of music had as much to do with his decision as my voice.

Speaking of Frederick M. Lehman's great hymn "The Love of God" reminds me of something I learned about it not long ago. Rumor had it that the third verse lyrics were found on the walls of an institution about the time this popular hymn was written in 1917. Though this could be true, the roots of it go back to the eleventh century, at least, and maybe further. According to my information, a modern-day translation of the verse was made by Rabbi Joseph Marcus from the Aramaic. A close approximation of the verse is used one day each year in the Jewish observance of *Shavuot* (Festival of Weeks) which begins seven weeks after Passover.

But without Mrs. Lehman there would be no song. Like Mother's habit of placing poems and notes on the piano for me, Frederick Lehman's wife put such findings in her husband's lunch pail. Mr. Lehman was a minister, but because most of his churches were small and could pay him little, he worked at various jobs to support his family. One of these jobs was in a cheese factory, and it was there that Mr. Lehman got his inspiration for "The Love of God." His wife had come into possession of a poem which began, "Could we with ink the ocean fill...." She put a copy of it in Frederick's lunch pail. He was so moved by the words that he came home that night and worked on a tune to go with them. Later, he wrote two other verses and thus was born another great gospel hymn.

Whatever the third verse's origin, it is good to know that Christians and Jews share in the sentiments expressed in these great words of praise to God:

>*1st verse*
>**The love of God is greater far**
>**Than tongue or pen can ever tell;**
>**It goes beyond the highest star,**
>**And reaches to the lowest hell.**
>**The guilty pair, bowed down with care,**
>**God gave His Son to win;**
>**His erring child, He reconciled,**
>**And pardoned from his sin.**
>
>*Chorus*
>**Oh, Love of God, how rich and pure!**
>**How measureless and strong!**
>**It shall forevermore endure —**
>**The saints' and angels' song.**
>
>*3rd verse*
>**Could we with ink the ocean fill,**
>**And were the skies of parchment made;**
>**Were every stalk on earth a quill,**
>**And every man a scribe by trade;**
>**To write the love of God above**
>**Would drain the ocean dry;**
>**Nor could the scroll contain the whole,**
>**Tho' stretched from sky to sky.**

After my time with Emerson Williams, I studied with Price Boone who sang tenor in the Calvary Baptist Church choir. An operatic talent, Price once seemed destined for a starring role at the Met, but after his Number One admirer and sponsor Herbert Witherspoon, Met general manager, died, interest in Price waned. He switched to teaching and I was one of his lucky pupils.

I sang in a quartet with Price on Erling C. Olsen's program, "Meditations in the Psalms," over WHN and WMCA. Others in that group were Hassie Mayfield, soprano, and William Miller, top tenor. Our theme song which we used to open and close the program was the eternally beautiful "When Morning Gilds the Skies."

>*When morning gilds the skies*
>*My heart awaking cries,*
>*May Jesus Christ be praised!*

Alike at work and prayer,
To Jesus I repair;
May Jesus Christ be praised!

In those days, Erma often provided skillful accompaniment for me. She studied piano at Toronto Conservatory and her musical ability was one of those additional blessings I got when she agreed to become my wife. I thank God for my girl, Erma, every day.

Another program I sang on at this time was J. Thurston Noé's "Sundown," which was aired each Friday evening. For a couple of years, I did two songs each week on his organ program. Mr. Noé was organist and director of the Calvary Baptist Church choir, a talented musician and composer. The theme of "Sundown" was Mr. Noé's own beloved "Thou Light of Light." Such a glorious benediction!

The sun goes down, the evening shadows lengthen,
The western hills are rimmed with golden light,
The day is o'er, the twilight glow is fading,
A silent tide flows out into the night.
Though still and deep, the darkness cannot hide Thee
Thou Light of light, shine through the night to me.

And I remember practicing with Mr. Noé and the Calvary choir at the church across from Carnegie Hall in preparation for special services, such as at Christmas or Easter. No one threw himself into rehearsals any more enthusiastically or more completely than he did. He was greatly praised for his conducting of Handel's *Messiah* and Dubois' *The Seven Last Words of Christ,* whenever he presented them. I remember in particular the time we did *The Seven Last Words* on network radio. What a production! In addition to some of the finest voices in New York, Mr. Noé had brought in several musicians from the Philharmonic to add to the grandeur. For a little more drama that night, he had arranged to have the lights turned out during the famous storm passage. Price Boone sang the tenor aria just before the storm.

Then, the cymbals crashed and the organ thundered. It was the most effective simulation of a storm I have ever heard. Mr. Noé directed the choir from the organ, his music lit by a small blue light. It was the only light in the church, and though dim, I could make out the expression on his face. How he was enjoying "his storm"!

Finally, *The Seven Last Words of Christ* reached that final crescendo:

Christ, we do all adore Thee
And we do praise Thee forever.

When it was over, I caught the triumphant look on Mr. Noé's face, a look I'll never forget. And there were tears in his eyes — he was so moved.

At rehearsal for that concert, I remember him telling me one day, "The basses need to come on a little stronger, with more confidence at this point. You lead them, Beverly. When I give you the signal, come in *fortissimo*."

I nodded that I would.

As we sang, Mr. Noé moved across the highly polished floor from one side of the area to the other, coaching the different sections. Just before the part he had mentioned to me, he was on the opposite side leading the sopranos. Suddenly, he turned and dashed in our direction, sliding the last ten feet like an ice skater. As he came to a skidding halt in front of me, he jabbed his index finger in my face and commanded, *"Now!"* I was so amused that I broke up as did everyone else in the choir — including Mr. Noé.

The last time I saw him was in Birmingham, Michigan, in 1967. I had a singing date at Detroit's Cobo Hall and I drove out from there to visit him. He and his wife had moved to Michigan to be near his son, Dick, who with some other engineers helped design the famous retractable hardtop for Ford. When I walked into his living room, one of the first things I saw was his Steinway grand piano. I recalled how I used to go out to the Noés' home in South Orange, New Jersey, with others and practice while he accompanied us. Such fantastic music he got out of that instrument, the same one he used to compose on.

We had a great time reminiscing that day. Though showing age, his spirit was still young. Once, he excused himself and went into another room to get some music to play for me. His wife, Mabel, whispered, "He's enjoying himself so much. He hasn't played the piano in over a year."

I couldn't imagine what would keep that lover of music away from his piano, but I learned when I got home where a letter from Mrs. Noé was waiting.

I did not know if I could stand to tell you when you were here, but we lost Dick a year ago. A sudden heart attack. It seemed so unnecessary for one so young...When there is only one there is such an awful void left.

Their son Dick was just forty-two when he died — on his father's birthday. I was even more pleased that I had been able to visit the Noés after receiving that letter.

A few months later news came from Mrs. Noé that "her Thurston" had died. I was on my way to Australia at the time, and though I talked with her by phone, I was not able to attend the funeral which I regretted.

When I got back home again, Mrs. Noé had a surprise for me. She wrote:

> One day I said, quite casually, not dreaming that he would pass first, "Thurston, what would you want me to do about the piano?" As you know he was always a little slow and deliberate in speaking, but he answered spontaneously and with that spark of pleasant temperament, "My one and only choice would be Bev Shea, but I don't know that he would want it."

Want it! I wrote back immediately to tell Mrs. Noé how honored I would be to have the piano, not only because I've always wanted a grand piano, but because it belonged to a dear friend who used it to compose many outstanding hymns of praise. Today, it occupies a prominent place in our home, and I use it often. I never sit down to play it but what I remember Thurston and the history that the piano represents.

While doing research for this book, I called Mrs. Noé and she kindly sent along a quotation from John Ruskin's *Ethics of the Dust*. It was a favorite of Thurston's and reflects his own personal philosophy, I think. The paper reads:

"Rest"

There is no music in a "rest," but there is the making of music in it.

In our whole life melody, the music is broken off here and there by "rests" and we foolishly think we have come to the end of the tune. God sends a time of forced leisure, sickness, disappointed plans, frustrated efforts that makes a sudden pause in the choral hymn of our lives, and we lament that our voice must be silent and our part missing in the music which ever goes up to the ear of the Creator.

How does the musician read the rest?

See him beat the time with unvarying count and catch up the next note true and steady as if no breaking place had come in between.

Not without design does God write the music of our lives. But be it ours to learn the time and not be dismayed at the "rests." They are not to be slurred over, not to be omitted, nor to destroy the melody, nor to change the keynote.

If we look up, God Himself will beat the time for us. With the eye on Him, we shall strike the next note full and clear.

At the bottom of it was an editorial comment by Thurston. He felt that the line which reads "God sends a time of forced leisure, etc...." should read, "There *seems* to be a time of forced leisure,..." Thurston's explanation: "We cannot believe a good God would send distress on His child when even a human father would refrain from doing so."

Interesting — how one friendship, one contact, one opportunity leads to another. Mr. Noé introduced me to Price Boone. With Price I sang on Erling C. Olsen's program. Among the guest speakers on that radio hour was Dr. Will Houghton, who after serving as minister at Calvary Baptist went to Chicago to serve as president of Moody Bible Institute. Dr. Houghton is an important link in my life because he was responsible for my entering full-time religious work.

At Pinebrook Bible Conference in the Poconos the summer of 1938, Dr. Houghton asked me if I had ever considered Christian radio as a vocation. I told him quite honestly that I hadn't.

"There's an opening on the staff of WMBI (the Moody Bible Institute Station in Chicago) that I think you could fill," he told me. Before the summer was over I had been hired and was on my way to Chicago.

My wife of four years, Erma — the Ottawa girl I'd courted with my violin — joined me a month later and we thus began a joint adventure that is now into its fourth decade. For the wonderful experiences that have followed that decision I can only respond:

> **Praise God from Whom all blessings flow,**
> **Praise Him, all creatures here below,**
> **Praise Him above, ye heavenly host,**
> **Praise Father, Son and Holy Ghost.**

3

A Full-Time Ministry of Song

The Christ of Every Road

There's a long road and a weary road
As it winds and twists along,
There are sad men who once were glad men,
But silent is their song,
Life is dead, they say
For He went away,
One in whom our hopes were borne,
He was by our side, then crucified,
Now we walk this road forlorn.

Those words were written by Dr. Houghton (the music by Wendell Loveless, former director of WMBI) who conducted a radio program each Sunday called "Let's Go Back to the Bible." Shortly after going to Chicago, I began singing regularly on that program. What a privilege it was to work with Dr. Houghton, a dedicated servant of Christ! In addition to doing "Let's Go Back to the Bible," I sang daily at 8:15 A.M. over WMBI on a program called "Hymns From the Chapel," as I mentioned before.

Occasionally some people stopped by the radio studios to say hello. One of them was a ministerial student at nearby Wheaton College. His name was Billy Graham.

It was only a short time later that I heard him speak — at a Chicago Youth for Christ Rally. That was an exciting night, really the launching of Youth for Christ by Torrey Johnson. A crowd of 2,900 showed up at Orchestra Hall on Michigan Avenue. I remember singing two spirituals that night, "Yes, He Did" and "The Old Time Religion." That young and ecumenical audience particularly liked some ad-libbing:

> **Give me that old time religion,**
> **Give me that old time religion,**
> **It's good enough for me —**
> **It makes the Baptists love the Methodists,**
> **Makes the Methodists love the Baptists,**
> **Makes the Presbyterians love — everybody.**

Billy's sermon was on his favorite subject: becoming a Christian. And he convinced a goodly number that it was a good time to do just that.

Meanwhile, I continued studying music (under Gino Monaco) and I was singing at various functions throughout the Midwest. In 1944 through my friendship with Bob Walker (now editor-publisher of *Christian Life)* who was on the board of Club Aluminum headed by Herbert J. Taylor, I was hired to do a daily, fifteen-minute show over WCFL. It was called "Club Time" and when I signed the contract for thirteen weeks it ended my association with WMBI. The station's policy prohibited employees from working commercially, so I had to resign. The move was a gamble, but Erma and I entered it prayerfully and it proved to be the right decision — again.

Eventually, the program went nationwide in September, 1945. It was aired weekly for seven years.

A feature of the show was doing the favorite hymn of a well-known person. I remember singing "In the Garden," Kate Smith's favorite, and "Softly and Tenderly" which was the favorite of my singing idol, John Charles Thomas. It's always been one of my top choices, too. Written by Will Thompson (known as the bard of Ohio) the noted composer once visited Dwight L. Moody near the end of the evangelist's life. Reaching up from his bed, Moody is said to have told Mr. Thompson, "Will, I would rather have written 'Softly and Tenderly' than anything I have been able to do in my whole life." Moody's appreciation of the hymn was prophetic. The relatively new work came to be one of the most popular invitational songs of all time.

> **Softly and tenderly Jesus is calling,**
> **Calling for you and for me,**
> **See on the portals He's waiting and watching,**
> **Watching for you and for me.**
>
> **Come home, come home,**
> **Ye who are weary, come home;**
> **Earnestly, tenderly, Jesus is calling,**
> **Calling, O sinner, come home!**

I started "Club Time" in 1944 about the same time I agreed to sing on a Sunday evening program called "Songs in the Night" over WCFL. Torrey Johnson had originated the program, but had to give it up because of pressing Youth for Christ commitments. His young prodigy, Billy Graham, who by now was pastor of The Village Church, Western Springs, Illinois, had agreed to succeed him.

Billy came to me and asked if I would sing on the program. Though overcommitted myself, I couldn't say no, especially when I learned that he had volunteered to go without salary in order to get his struggling church to sponsor the program. It was a decision I've never regretted. The name of the program came from that verse in Job 35:10. Forsaken, Job cried out, *Where is God my maker, who giveth songs in the night?*

Each Sunday night a group known as the King's Carolers and I would open the program from Western Springs by singing Wendell P. Loveless' "Songs in the Night."

> **Songs in the night,**
> **The Lord giveth songs in the night,**
> **Sorrows may come, darkness or light**
> **But He giveth songs in the night.**

This is not to be confused with another song which bears the same title. It was written by J. Thurston Noé and Dr. Houghton.

> **What though the hours be long and dreary,**
> **What though the road be hard and weary,**
> **Songs in the night, I'll not fear sorrow,**
> **Songs in the night, and then tomorrow,**
> **The world holds but darkness and Christ is the light,**
> **He giveth songs, songs in the night.**

Those were exciting days but only a shadow of things to come. For Billy Graham there was Youth for Christ work which followed his pastorate at Western Springs. This new endeavor took him all over the country and — in 1946 — on a six-month campaign in the British Isles. His song leader for those meetings was a young handsome package of energy named Cliff Barrows.

Upon their return, I received an invitation from Billy to join him, Cliff, and an old classmate of Billy's — Grady Wilson — in Charlotte, North Carolina, in November, 1947, for a three-week city-wide rally. I agreed and the foundation for the Crusade work was laid that November in the First Baptist Church on Tryon Street. The crowds were such that we had to move to the armory the final week. The first number I did there — the unofficial launching of the Crusades — was one of Billy's favorites, "I Will Sing the Wondrous Story."

> I will sing the wondrous story
>   Of the Christ who died for me
> Sing it with the saints in glory
>   Gathered by the crystal sea.

Meanwhile, I continued my work in Chicago, concentrating on "Club Time." I joined Billy, Cliff, and Grady for about three campaigns a year in those early days, but it was not until September of 1949 that Billy's ministry took wings. The springboard proved to be the Los Angeles Crusade.

There, in a huge tent at Washington Boulevard and Hill Street, six thousand people came nightly. The three-week campaign stretched to eight and I sang each night, which took some doing. I had to return to Chicago after Monday's service, fly all night, do my "Club Time" stint live on Tuesday morning, then get on a plane and fly all day to get back in time for Tuesday night's service. It was an exhausting schedule, but well worth it.

Some of the people who came forward at the Los Angeles Crusade were famous, and these men and women created news which spread and attracted others. One of those people was a famous personality and songwriter who, after he found Christ, wrote these well-known words:

> It is no secret what God can do,
> What He did for others, He'll do for you.

The author, as most know, is Stuart Hamblen.

Stuart figured in my joining RCA a short time later. We were on the same program at Convention Hall in Philadelphia, and the following morning before we headed our separate ways he told me he had been talking to some RCA people about putting me under contract.

"You aren't under contract with anyone else, are you?"

"No. I do have a couple of records which are distributed by the Singspiration people, but I'm not under contract."

A few weeks later I was though, and, in the spring of 1951, I recorded *Inspiration Songs.* "It Is No Secret" was included because I liked it so much and because I wanted to say thanks to Stuart. Also on that album were "Ivory Palaces," "Known Only to Him," "Tenderly He Watches" and "If You Know the Lord," by Bickley Reichner which I got to introduce.

> **If you know the Lord,**
> **You need nobody else,**
> **To see you through the darkest night.**
> **You can walk alone,**
> **You only need the Lord,**
> **He'll keep you on the road marked right.**

I'll never forget that first recording session. The famous Hugo Winterhalter Orchestra provided the accompaniment and I was so nervous I couldn't do anything right. Finally, Steve Sholes got me on track and I managed to get the album recorded. It proved to be a very successful one, still being distributed. The RCA people called the album, No. 1187, "Old Faithful," and they continue to make it available.

It wasn't long before "Club Time" rang down the curtain on seven years of programs. A short time later, I finished eight years on "Songs in the Night." Providentially, I believe, that work was ended to make way for the adventure ahead with the Billy Graham Evangelistic Association. Soon came the "Hour of Decision" radio broadcasts, evenings of sacred concerts, Crusade work all over the world, and a ministry through records.

It still seems like a dream.

4

Around the World with Song

The excitement that encompassed people who were a part of the Billy Graham team in those early years is hard to capture in words. So many dramatic things happened.

How the "Hour of Decision" came into being in 1950 has been told so often it doesn't need repeating. Enough to say, that the manner in which people responded with financial help to assure the program's first thirteen weeks on ABC was nothing short of miraculous.

I'll never forget the first program carried over 150 stations. We were holding a Crusade in Atlanta and we did the first show live. What electricity filled the air! Cliff emceed and led the singing. Jerry Beavan read the Crusade news report, which featured some of the exciting events happening. Grady read Scripture. I sang "I'd Rather Have Jesus" and Billy gave a stirring message.

Then, we sat back to await the verdict.

There were skeptics who thought the program would fail.

Others thought it would be just so-so, reaching the already churched, missing the unsaved, but approval of the program was not long in coming. In five weeks, it had the largest audience of any religious program in history — reaching more people, some speculated, in a single night than D. L. Moody had spoken to in his lifetime.

Billy's Spirit-filled and Spirit-directed sermons are the lifeblood of the program, of course, but music has also played a significant role. Cliff's part in selecting music, directing choirs, and producing the "Hour of Decision" has been crucial to its success. I have been privileged to be a part of the musical team, and have been blessed immeasurably.

The mail I've received from listeners of the "Hour of Decision" has been so gratifying — not because I have been a singer on the program but because there is great power in song messages. Dr. William Pentecost was not the first to recognize the efficacy of song but he made a poignant observation:

"I am profoundly sure," he wrote, "that among the ordained instrumentalists for the conversion and sanctification of the soul, God has not given a greater one, beside the preaching of the Gospel, than the singing of psalms and hymns and spiritual songs." Dwight L. Moody was as enthusiastic about the "singing of the Gospel" and was one of the first to recognize the ability of spiritual music to reach men's hearts — even though he could not carry a tune himself.

In one of the more humorous stories in George Stebbins' book, he writes about Mr. Moody's problem:

> I first thought (the discordant sound) was caused by something wrong with the organ...I listened to see if there might be one of the notes sounding when it ought to be silent, and found the discords were not from that source.
>
> I was not long in doubt, however, for I soon heard the voice of Mr. Moody singing away as heartily as you please with no more idea of tune or time than a child. I then learned for the first time that he was one of the unfortunates who have no sense of pitch or harmony, and hence unable to recognize one tune from another...in spite of that defect, he...loved the sound of music and I have seen him...bowed under the power of an impressive hymn as I have known no other to be.

I would not be one to tell tales out of school, but a well-known evangelist friend of mine with whom I've been associated over twenty-five years has been afflicted with Mr. Moody's problem — the malady of no melody. This friend has a beautifully sonorous speaking voice and most would imagine an equally good singing voice, but it is not the case. Nonetheless, like Mr. Moody, he appreciates the power of a gospel song and he, too, joins in heartily.

My mail tells me time and again of the people who have been touched by gospel music. Seldom does a batch of letters fail to include a note from someone who has been helped through a serious problem by the message of a spiritual song.

From Australia comes a letter from a woman contemplating suicide who was dissuaded when she heard "I'd Rather Have Jesus" on the "Hour of Decision." From Colorado, a letter from a man who heard a selection from a recent album over radio. The song, "He Will Hold Me Fast," gave him reassurance to face the future without his wife who had died of cancer. From California, a young housewife wrote me recently:

I cannot afford a record player or records, but I hear you sing often over my little radio. Thank God for your ministry of song. Music has a way of lifting my spirits, especially gospel music. I heard you sing once at a nearby church and at that time you told us about your mother's favorite song, "Singing I Go." It has become my theme song. As you told us through song that night, "Jesus has lifted my load." Since then, I sing it whenever I'm feeling low and you were right, He does lift my load.

A woman from the South wrote me last January:

For Christmas I received one of your records, but as my husband was very ill, I didn't play it. After his death and funeral a few weeks later, I came home to an empty house and for want of some sound to fill the void, I put your record on the phonograph. The first words I heard were, 'I know not what the future holds, but I know who holds the future.' It was all I needed. I turned off the music. Divine strength swept over me and *light* came to me. It was a miracle how I went through that day. Thank God for the hymns of faith.

From a woman in the Midwest who attended one of our evenings of sacred songs:

Thank you, your pianist and your organization for bringing us a great sermon in song. A friend of my husband's who had lost all interest in the church came along to the program to please his wife. He was so moved he said he plans to begin attending church again.

Last week a letter from Maine came from a woman who had just received news her mother was dying in a distant state:

I couldn't go home and was heartbroken. My husband, on his way home from work, had the car radio on and he heard you singing a wonderful song called "Tenderly He Watches." He knew the words were just the ones I needed to hear so he drove several miles to get the record for me. I played it over and over and it sustained me through this difficult time. How great it is to know that through any ordeal, tenderly He watches over us.

Probably the most heartening letter I have received recently came from a young mother who lives behind the Iron Curtain. Her son is a voice student and wanted to sing gospel music, but they wrote me that none was available in their country. I sent a couple of records that got through. When the boy told his teacher that he wanted to sing gospel music, she didn't know what he meant. The mother wrote:

> Then, God gives to Eddie's mind to ask her if she has gramaphone, he will bring her some records that she can know which kind of songs he wish to learn. She knows English and German language. When she heard the records, she was so happy she was playing all day during nearly one month. They liked "The Love of God" so much they translated it and then are singing so loud that the windows was trembling. Can you imagine what great courage she has singing this Christians songs by opened window? Her house is on main street and everyone who passes hear the beautiful song. Eddie says she was jumping on her chair from happiness, playing piano and singing, telling: wonderful, wonderful.

I include these letter excerpts not because they reflect kindly on the singer, but that they testify again to the timeless power of gospel music and hymns to reach people and change lives.

Through recordings and radio programs such as the "Hour of Decision," our songs were soon reaching the far corners of the earth, and as the Crusade work grew I was privileged to visit many of these places in person.

One of our early trips was to England in 1949. It was on this trip that I learned the story behind Ira D. Sankey's "The Ninety and Nine," and though I have heard it told many times since, I had never read Sankey's account of it until Fred Bauer and I began to work on this book. In his book *Sankey's Story of the Gospel Hymns,* published in 1906 by the Philadelphia-based Sunday School Times Company, he wrote:

> It was in the year 1874 that the poem, "The Ninety and Nine," was discovered, set to music, and sent out upon its world-wide mission. Its discovery seemed as if by chance, but I cannot regard it otherwise than providential. Mr. Moody had just been conducting a series of meetings in Glasgow, and I had been assisting him in his work as director of the singing. We were at the railway station at Glasgow and about to take the train for Edinburgh, whither we were going upon an urgent invitation of ministers to hold three days of meetings there before going into the Highlands. We had held a three months' series in Edinburgh just previous to our four months' campaign in Glasgow. As we were about to board the train I bought a weekly newspaper, for a penny. Being much fatigued by our incessant labors at Glasgow, and

intending to begin work immediately upon our arrival at Edinburgh, we did not travel second- or third-class, as was our custom, but sought the seclusion and rest which a first-class railway carriage in Great Britain affords. In the hope of finding news from America I began perusing my lately purchased newspaper. This hope, however, was doomed to disappointment, as the only thing in its columns to remind an American of home and native land was a sermon by Henry Ward Beecher.

I threw the paper down, but shortly before arriving in Edinburgh I picked it up again with a view to reading the advertisements. While thus engaged my eyes fell upon a little piece of poetry in a corner of the paper. I carefully read it over, and at once made up my mind that this would make a great hymn for evangelistic work — if it had a tune. So impressed was I that I called Mr. Moody's attention to it, and he asked me to read it to him. This I proceeded to do with all the vim and energy at my command. After I had finished I looked at my friend Moody to see what the effect had been, only to discover that he had not heard a word, so absorbed was he in a letter which he had received from Chicago. My chagrin can be better imagined than described. Notwithstanding this experience, I cut out the poem and placed it in my musical scrap book — which, by the way, has been the seedplot from which sprang many of the Gospel songs that are now known throughout the world.

At the noon meeting on the second day, held at the Free Assembly Hall, the subject presented by Mr. Moody and other speakers was "The Good Shepherd." When Mr. Moody had finished speaking he called upon Dr. Bonar to say a few words. He spoke only a few minutes, but with great power, thrilling the immense audience by his fervid eloquence. At the conclusion of Dr. Bonar's words Mr. Moody turned to me with the question, "Have you a solo appropriate for this subject, with which to close the service?" I had nothing suitable in mind, and was greatly troubled to know what to do. The Twenty-third Psalm occurred to me, but this had been sung several times in the meeting. I knew that every Scotsman in the audience would join me if I sang that, so I could not possibly render this favorite psalm as a solo. At this moment I seemed to hear a voice saying: "Sing the hymn you found on the train!" But I thought this impossible, as no music had ever been written for that hymn. Again the impression came strongly upon me that I must sing the beautiful and appropriate words I had found the day before, and placing the little newspaper slip on the organ in front of me, I lifted my heart in prayer, asking God to help me so to sing that the people might hear and understand. Laying my hands upon the organ I struck the key of A flat, and began to sing.

Note by note the tune was given, which has not been changed from that day to this. As the singing ceased a great sigh seemed to go up from the meeting, and I knew that the song had reached the hearts of my Scots audience. Mr. Moody was greatly moved. Leaving the pulpit, he came down to where I was seated. Leaning over the organ, he looked at the little newspaper slip from which the song had been sung, and with tears in his eyes said: "Sankey, where did you get that hymn? I never heard the like of it in my life." I was also moved to tears and arose and replied: "Mr. Moody, that's the hymn I read to you yesterday on the train, which you did not hear." Then Mr. Moody raised his hand and pronounced the benediction, and the meeting closed. Thus "The Ninety and Nine" was born.

While visiting a mission (Carrubbers Close Mission in Edinburgh) Cliff Barrows and I were taken into a building and shown the very reed organ on which Sankey had composed the music for Elizabeth C. Clephane's poem. Invited to play it (the Scots call it a "Kist o'whustles") I picked out "The Ninety and Nine" from memory. It was a moving experience.

A few years later the mission gave the organ to the Billy Graham Evangelistic Association and it is now kept in the chapel of our head-quarters building in Minneapolis. One time while I was visiting there, I participated in a service and sang "The Ninety and Nine" accompanying myself with that famous instrument. If you ever visit the BGEA offices in Minneapolis, be sure to look for Sankey's little organ. It will soon be 100 years since he first played that classic on it.

Mr. Sankey's book, which was written in 1906 — two years before he died — contains so much interesting hymn nostalgia. In addition to stories behind the writing of many all-time gospel songs written by friends and aquaintances, Sankey talks about the origin of some of his own compositions, such as "I Am Praying for You," "Faith Is the Victory," "Jesus, I will Trust Thee," "Hiding in Thee," and "There'll Be No Dark Valley."

He also talks about his long singing ministry in the company of Dwight L. Moody. In particular, I was moved in reading about his recollection of Mr. Moody's invitation to Sankey to join him, Sankey's hesitation, Moody's prayerful insistence, the vocalist's capitulation. He also talks about the many campaigns in which he shared the platform with the famed evangelist. In one passage, he relates that when Mr. Moody went on his second speaking trip to England in 1872, he (Sankey) was left in charge of the Tabernacle (in Chicago) "assisted by Major Whittle, Richard Thain, Fleming H. Revell and others." Of course, Mr. Revell was the founder of the company which is the publisher of this book. He began the Fleming H. Revell Company in 1870 by publishing a collection of Moody's sermons.

There are many anecdotes of fascination in the book, but no story is quite so steeped in history as his account of the Chicago Fire, Sunday,

October 8, 1871. According to Sankey, he was participating with Moody in services at Farwell Hall, and on this Sunday night Mr. Moody had just finished his sermon and had asked Sankey to sing "Today the Saviour Calls." Sankey had reached the third verse of that hymn...

> **Today the Saviour calls:**
> **For refuge fly;**
> **The storm of justice falls,**
> **And death is nigh...**

when he reports, "My voice was drowned by the loud noise of fire engines rushing past the hall and the tolling of bells." Mr. Moody immediately dismissed the congregation and all went out into the streets. Moody and Sankey stood for a moment looking at the ominous glow, then they separated — Sankey going across the river in the direction of the fire to offer his assistance, and Moody to his family on the north side. It was the last time they were to see each other for two months.

Sankey reports that the rapidly progressing fire soon drove him back across the river to Farwell Hall, which was soon to be consumed by fire. He gathered some of his most important possessions together in suitcases and tried to move them a half a mile's distance to Lake Michigan, but could find no transportation available so made two trips. Along the way, he assisted others to the water's edge and urged many people out of their apartments. He recalled that some "laughed me to scorn." Eventually, he took refuge in a boat until the fire had burned itself out. Then he made his way home to his family in Pennsylvania by rail. It was several days before he learned by wire that Moody and his family also had escaped the flames.

It was on another trip to England for our London Crusade at Harringay Arena in 1954 that I came upon a newly translated hymn which was to become one of the favorites of our day — "How Great Thou Art." Though I didn't know the background then, I was to learn later the history of the song from its translator, S. K. Hine, an English missionary. The circuitous route it traveled to fame is most fascinating. Born in Sweden (and christened "O Great God") in 1885 at the hand of a preacher and editor named Carl Boberg, it was translated into German (by a man named Manfred von Glehn of Estonia) in 1907. Then it went into Russian (translated by the Martin Luther of that country, Ivan S. Prokhanoff) in 1912. "How Great Thou Art" was put into English in 1925, but under the title "O Mighty God." Finally, in 1948, another translation was made from the Russian to the English (this time by Mr. Hine) and that version was entitled

"How Great Thou Art." Mr. Hine included it in a magazine he published and people around the world wrote for copies. He obligingly made reprints and it was one of those copies that I was handed in 1954.

The poll in the front of this book showing it to be fourth on the all-time favorite list is not surprising to me. It is deserving of its esteem because it uplifts all who hear it.

In the days since, it has become one of my most requested hymns along with "I'd Rather Have Jesus." During the 1957 New York Crusade, I sang it over a hundred times. I also have recorded it three times for RCA and it has been used scores of times on the "Hour of Decision."

England figures in the story behind a hymn I wrote in 1955, "The Wonder of It All." I was on my way to Scotland for meetings there aboard the S.S. *United States* bound for Southampton when inspiration came from conversation with another passenger. He wanted to know what went on at our meetings and after detailing the sequence of things at a typical Billy Graham Crusade meeting, I found myself at a loss for words when I tried to describe the response that usually accompanied Mr. Graham's invitation to become a Christian. "What happens then never becomes commonplace ... watching people by the hundreds come forward ... oh, if you could just see the wonder of it all."

"I think I should," he answered. Then, he wrote these words on a card and handed it back to me: THE WONDER OF IT ALL.

"That sounds like a song to me." Later that night, I wrote words on that theme and roughed out a melody to go with them. Since then, I've recorded "The Wonder of It All" and am happy to say that many other vocalists have recorded it, too.

I didn't think a great deal of it at first. For one thing I couldn't get one section to rhyme. That night on the ship I wrote:

> **The wonder of sunset at evening,**
> **The wonder of sunrise at morn,**
> **But the wonder of wonders that thrills my soul,**
> **Is the wonder that God loves me.**

In Minneapolis a few months later for an engagement at the First Baptist Church, I told my friend Dr. Curtis B. Akenson about the experience and he encouraged me to sing it. I was reluctant and told the congregation so.

"Some of it doesn't rhyme."

It didn't matter apparently, because they responded enthusiastically to it and a few days later I called Cindy Walker, a dear
friend from Texas, whose song-writing talent has put her name
among the greats of today — both in religious and pop music. When I
told her about my problem, she had a solution inside of a minute.

"How about this, Bev?" she advised.

The Wonder of It All

There's the wonder of sunset at evening —
The wonder as sunrise I see.
But the wonder of wonders that thrills my soul
Is the wonder that God loves me.

There's the wonder of springtime and harvest —
The sky — the stars — the sun.
But the wonder of wonders that thrills my soul
Is a wonder that's only begun.

The wonder of sunset at evening,
The wonder of sunrise I *see,*
But the wonder of wonders that thrills my soul
Is the wonder that God loves me.

And that's how it was published, thanks to a real songwriter, Cindy
Walker!

After I had recorded it, Joe Blinco, a Britisher who was an associate evangelist on the Billy Graham team for many years, told me it
was one of the most meaningful hymns he'd ever heard. I thanked
him, thinking he was showing characteristic kindness, but I learned
differently. Near the end of his life, he became the director of Forest
Home in the High Sierras. It is a spiritual center established by the
late Dr. Henrietta Mears for the young people of the Hollywood
Presbyterian Church.

When Joe died, many of us went there for his funeral and I was
pleased to have a part in honoring this great servant of God's. On my
way into the chapel, I passed a tree that had been planted for him. On
a bronze plaque at its base were these words: JOE BLINCO — THE
WONDER OF IT ALL.

Travel is said to be broadening. It also has figured in the writing of
many hymns. People on trips — planes, trains, ships; in strange places
— have often been inspired to write.

I have had a couple of hymn writing experiences that happened while I was "on the road." In 1968 while participating in services in Australia, I was feeling rather blue one night, lonesome for family and home. Picking up my Bible which I always carry in my suitcase, I turned to John and read:

> Peace I leave with you, my peace I give unto you; not as the world giveth, give I unto you. Let not your heart be troubled, neither let it be afraid. (John 14:27)

As I read, music came to me. I was reassured and uplifted. Taking a pencil in hand, I wrote notes around these words:

> **Let not your heart be troubled,**
> **Neither let it be afraid,**
> **My peace I leave with you,**
> **My peace I leave with you,**
> **Not as the world giveth,**
> **Not as the world giveth,**
> **My peace I leave with you.**

Arthur Smith of Charlotte, North Carolina, took it from there. On a visit with him a short time later, he worked from my refrain, wrote verses for it, added a melody to his words and "Let Not Your Heart Be Troubled" was the result. I believe it was on that same visit that Arthur showed me a wonderful new composition of his which I have since recorded. Taking out his guitar (you may remember a pop tune called "Guitar Boogie" — well, he wrote it), he played and sang:

> **Acres of diamonds, mountains of gold,**
> **Rivers of silver, jewels untold;**
> **All these together, wouldn't buy you or me**
> **Peace when we're sleeping or a conscience that's free.**
> **A heart that's contented, a satisfied mind,**
> **These are the treasures money can't buy;**
> **If you have Jesus, there's more wealth in your soul,**
> **Than acres of diamonds, mountains of gold.**

Though the words came to me unsolicited and I wrote the music at home, the hymn "Blue Galilee" resulted in a travel experience recently. Erma and I visited the Holy Land in the spring of 1971 with a group of eighty-nine people led by Roy Gustafson, a most knowledgeable guide and Bible scholar. It was such a wonderful experience visiting the significant places mentioned in the Scriptures.

One afternoon during the trip, we boarded a ship to travel from Tiberias to a kibbutz across the Sea of Galilee. By previous arrangement, a cassette recording of "Blue Galilee" was taken on board for playing. Midway across, the ship's captain shut down the engines and that recording I'd made some time before came over the ship's loudspeakers.

Roy said, "Maybe we can get Bev to sing along with it." And I did.

I will not soon forget the picture of our ship drifting through that beautiful sea. Later, the captain (M. A. Ezekiel) told me he would like a copy of the recording.

"It's so appropriate," he said. "I'd like to play it for all my passengers in the future."

Maybe it is the change of scenery which inspires music. While Fred Bauer and I were working on this book, I was fiddling with the lyrics to a song which had been going through my head, but hadn't quite jelled. Then, Fred went with me to open the Shea summer cabin in Quebec (there's no phone there and we figured we could get in a couple of uninterrupted days on the manuscript). In that beautiful setting, I began revising the words to a song I've named "I Will Praise Him." I'm still not satisfied with it, but if it comes to anything that retreat will have figured in the result. (It is included in a recent album entitled "I'd Rather Have Jesus.") We used to go to a lake west of Ottawa as the guest of the Hibbert Vipond family. The Viponds are old friends of my family. Then one summer Hibbert said, "Bev, why not build a place here. I've got just the spot for you." He showed me a little island in a cove not far from his home on the water. "It's yours if you want it," he said. Erma and I were overjoyed.

It was characteristic generosity (his son and daughter-in-law, Denzil and Joy, are themselves just as giving). Anyway, we put up a small prefab, and the cabin has given the Shea family some wonderful memories.

Sometimes in traveling around the world, language becomes a barrier, and because I'm still trying to master English, I haven't had much success with some of the others. I remember a trip we made through Europe in 1955, visiting several different countries. In preparation for the tour, I attempted to learn at least one song in the language of each country on our itinerary. For example, I learned — phonetically — "Pass Me Not, O Gentle Savior" in German, "He the Pearly Gates Will Open" in Swedish, and "I'd Rather Have Jesus" in Finnish. Though I'm sure my accent and pronunciation left something to be desired in each case, the audiences seemed to appreciate the attempts.

But the most vivid memory is our sailing out of Helsinki, Finland, following our meeting there. Many of the committee which had labored so hard to make the visit a success came to the ship to see us off.

From the pier they called up to me, "Sing 'I'd Rather Have Jesus' again in our tongue." Fortunately, I had the phonetic version in my pocket. Handing it to Tedd Smith, he held the paper while I cupped my hands and sang. It was a meaningful way for me to say "goodbye" to some wonderful friends.

Not all my attempts with another tongue proved as successful, however. I tried to do "The Love of God" in French in Paris at Villedrôme d'hiver, but flubbed up despite David Barnes' coaching. The next day, Cliff — ever the diplomat — said, "You know, Bev, I understand that here in France the man on the street knows many of the spirituals in English. I think you could do the spirituals here in English and get them across."

"Cliff, my friend," I told him, "I know what you are trying to say, and I agree with you, buddy." When I was growing up in Canada I heard a lot of beautiful French spoken — but not by me.

On this same trip, we visited many U.S. service installations and a documentary film entitled *Battleground Europe* was shot. I noted that the cameramen were around shooting footage each time I sang one of my translations. I thought that would provide some interesting sequences, but when the documentary came out, none of the "language" numbers were included. For my solo in the film, they used "Roll, Jordan, Roll." C'est la vie!

Another time, World Wide Pictures — which has produced such films as *Oil Town U.S.A., The Restless Ones, Two A Penny, Mr. Texas, Souls in Conflict,* and *His Land* in addition to several documentaries — was filming a Crusade through Alabama. I remember we had lots of rain on the trip and one night in the football stadium at the University of Alabama, there was a terrible storm. To keep us dry on the platform, they covered us with a ghostly looking plastic, which kept whipping eerily in the wind. Not content with that, our beloved Grady Wilson sat under an umbrella, which proved unwise. It pierced the plastic and was a target for the next bolt of lightning. Grady, though unhurt, was one of the first off the platform when the state police suggested we'd better "move out."

The crowd all gathered under the stands, and while waiting out the rain, Cliff conducted an informal song service. Someone called, "Bev, sing 'The Old Rugged Cross.' " I answered, "I will if you all hum along." And so we began.

While I was singing I noticed the World Wide cameramen shooting the scene, hundreds of people huddled together as if in the catacombs singing "The Old Rugged Cross."

Afterward, Frank Jacobson, producer of the documentary commented, "I hope we got this on film. It was very moving."

I looked forward to seeing it on the documentary. But it was left on the cutting room floor, too. My song in the film was again "Roll, Jordan, Roll." Just call me Johnny One Note.

In the course of my travels, it's been my pleasant duty to sing before the President of the United States — twice each before Presidents Eisenhower, Johnson and Nixon. Twice the event was the Presidential Prayer Breakfast in Washington.

The first time was impromptu in 1954, when I was asked to lead those gathered in one of my favorites:

> **What a friend we have in Jesus**
> **All our sins and griefs to bear!**
> **What a privilege to carry**
> **Everything to God in prayer!**
>
> **Oh, what peace we often forfeit**
> **Oh, what needless pain we bear,**
> **All because we do not carry,**
> **Everything to God in prayer!**

My surprise came the next morning when (dressed in an old bathrobe and slippers) I sat down to breakfast with Erma back home. As the TV in the kitchen came into focus whom should I see on the "Today Show" but old psalm singer Shea — singing his heart out. And on his right stood the President joining in. He knew the words, no question about that.

A few months later, I was invited to the National Christian Endeavor's annual convention in Washington. Though President Eisenhower was expected to put in an appearance and make a few brief remarks, I doubted he would be present when I sang. However, he lingered afterward and was on hand when I sang "I'd Rather Have Jesus." Before he left he shook my hand and said:

"Thank you for that song."

I was deeply touched.

The most recent experience in which I was privileged to sing before a President came in January, 1969, at the White House. Mr. Nixon had just been inaugurated and had invited Billy Graham to conduct the first Sunday religious service in the East Room. Billy asked T. W. Wilson (Grady's brother), Tedd Smith and me to go with him and take part in the service. I sang "How Great Thou Art" that day. And though the service was impressive, some of the events leading up to it remain more vivid in my memory. We went to the White House early that day to have breakfast with the President, Mrs. Nixon, and their daughter, Tricia, in their private quarters. They were so warm and casual. Mrs. Nixon sat at my left, Tricia at my right. On around the table were Billy and Ruth Graham, Tedd, T. W., and the President.

The conversation was light and in a good-natured vein all through the meal. After breakfast, Mrs. Nixon showed us around the White House while Billy and the President went off to discuss the details of the service, but we regrouped with time to spare. While waiting for those invited to the service to arrive, the President went to a nearby grand piano and began playing — very well. But it was not his skill but his selection which took me by surprise. It was "He Will Hold Me Fast." As I stood nearby, I began humming.

"Do you know it?" he asked.

"Yes, I sang it as a boy."

I wondered where a man with Quaker roots had learned such an old-time hymn. Not long ago I think I got the answer. He learned the hymn at the Church of the Open Door in Los Angeles. When the President was a boy, I understand he attended a series of services conducted there by the Reverend Paul Rader, whose theme song happened to be "He Will Hold Me Fast."

> **When I fear my faith will fail**
> **Christ will hold me fast:**
> **When the tempter would prevail,**
> **He can hold me fast.**
>
> **He will hold me fast,**
> **For my Saviour loves me so,**
> **He will hold me fast.**

Not long after that, I recorded it for RCA and when the liner copy (comments on the back about the album) was being prepared I was asked about the hymn. When I told the writer why I'd included it, he wanted to use the story, but I vetoed the idea, thinking it would be presumptuous to make such speculation without more substantiation. I include the story here only because I have space to explain that it is speculation.

(Incidentally, President Nixon was sent a copy of that album *These Are the Things that Matter* and he responded appreciatively.)

I am privy to many fascinating events thanks to Billy who graciously includes me often. For instance, I went with him to Plymouth, Massachusetts, in December, 1970, for the 350th anniversary of the Mayflower landing, and sang on the program. When I accepted the invitation, I was interested to see that Norman Clayton was to lead the choir. Our paths first crossed in 1943 when I was helping Jack Wyrtzen in New York. Norman was working for Thomas Bakeries, the English muffin people, then — writing gospel music in his spare time. It was Jack who encouraged him to publish some of his compositions and Norman put together a book from scratch — typesetting, printing, and binding. I hadn't seen him in some time, so I was anticipating the reunion. Norman, as many of you know, is an accomplished composer, who wrote one of my first-line favorites, "If We Could See Beyond Today."

However, when I got to Plymouth the man who was conducting the music was not the one I expected. It was Norman, Jr. If that didn't make me look in the mirror for gray hairs! But like his father, he has wonderful musical talent and did a great job that day.

I sang two songs. One was entitled "O God, Beneath Thy Guiding Hand," a number I've had in my little black book for many years, and its lyrics were certainly appropriate. Unfortunately, the tune was not particularly strong, so I worked on a new one for the occasion.

> O God, beneath Thy guiding hand
> Our exiled fathers crossed the sea;
> And when they trod the wintry strand,
> With prayer and psalm they worshipped Thee.
>
> Thou heard'st (You heard) well-pleased, the song, the prayer;
> Thy blessing came, and still its power
> Shall onward through all ages, bear
> The memory of that holy hour.
>
> Laws, freedom, truth and faith in God
> Came with those exiles o'er the waves;
> And where their pilgrim feet have trod
> The God they trusted guards their graves (guarded their days)

> And here Thy name, O God of love,
> Their children's children shall adore,
> Till these eternal hills remove,
> And spring adorns the earth no more.

For the second selection, I chose "Take Time to Pray," a hymn recorded in 1952 on my second album. It also had words that fit. They hold a message for us all:

> I've been going my way
> Living life day by day
> Never thinking or stopping to pray
> Till the storm clouds came near
> Taking loved ones so dear.
> Now I'm trying to live God's way.
>
> Take time to pray,
> Bow your head in prayer every day
> Oh, please, dear God, please keep us free
> For you know what this land means to me.
> Take time to pray, never let me, O Lord, go astray
> Though the world may look dark and my soul holdeth fear
> Let me know, dear Lord, thou art near.

Special occasions require special attention be given to the selection of numbers, and I always try to give a great deal of prayer to the choices. One of my most memorable Christmases was spent in Vietnam in 1966. We were at An Khe for Christmas Eve, caught in a rainstorm that didn't look as if it was going to stop in time for the service, but it did and we had a wonderful meeting. On that occasion I chose that old favorite composed by Longfellow, "I Heard the Bells on Christmas Day" ...

> Then pealed the bells more loud and deep:
> "God is not dead, nor doth He sleep,
> The wrong shall fail, the right prevail
> With peace on earth, good will to men."

Of course, the standards at Christmas are always good choices. That same service was closed by Cliff leading everyone in "Silent Night." A Catholic chaplain had given each soldier a paper cup with a candle in it and just before we sang that blessed Christmas hymn, we all lit our candles. It was a beautiful sight.

The story behind "Silent Night" has always been one of my favorites, and though I have seen many tellings of it, none is more beautiful than one I read in *Guideposts* magazine's annual Christmas booklet several years ago. Glenn D. Kittler told it like this:

> Sadly the young pastor strolled through the snow-covered slopes above the village of Oberndorf, Austria. In a few days it would be Christmas Eve, but Josef Mohr knew there would be no music in his church to herald the great event. The new organ had broken down.
>
> Pausing, Pastor Mohr gazed at the scattered lights in the village below. The sight of the peaceful town, huddled warmly in the foothills, stirred his imagination. Surely it was on such a clear and quiet night as this that hosts of angels sang out the glorious news that the Saviour had been born.
>
> The young cleric sighed heavily as he thought, "If only we here in Oberndorf could celebrate the birth of Jesus with glorious music like the shepherds heard on that wonderful night."
>
> Standing there, his mind filled with visions of the first Christmas, Josef Mohr suddenly became aware that disappointment was fading from his heart; in its place surged a great joy. Vividly, he saw the manger, carved from a mountainside; he saw Mary and Joseph and the Child; he saw the strangers who had been attracted by the light of the great star. The image seemed to shape itself into the words of a poem.
>
> The next day he showed the poem to Franz Gruber, the church organist, who said, "These words should be sung at Christmas. But what could we use for accompaniment? This?" Glumly, he held up his guitar.
>
> The pastor replied, "Like Mary and Joseph in the stable, we must be content with what God provides for us."
>
> Franz Gruber studied the poem, then softly strummed the melody that came to him. Next he put the words to the melody and sang them. When he finished, his soul was ablaze with its beauty.
>
> On Christmas Eve, 1818, in a small Austrian village, the Oberndorf choir, accompanied only by a guitar, sang for the first time the immortal hymn that begins, "Silent Night,...Holy Night."

I remember another moving experience that Christmas — hearing Anita Bryant's rendition of "The Battle Hymn of the Republic" sung before an audience of 10,000 soldiers. Bob Hope's show had gotten its usual roaring reception. It had the expected number of beautiful girls clad in the expectedly stunning costumes. They sang and danced to the expected chorus of cheers and wolf whistles. But none of their applause matched that they gave to Anita when she concluded the program with that great Civil War hymn. I have seldom heard anything to rival their response. Deafening. And no one performs it as dramatically as Anita.

Like other majestic hymns in that category ("How Great Thou Art," "You'll Never Walk Alone," and the like) it has lyrics that bring goose pimples to the spine. It was written in 1861 by Julia Ward Howe, a dedicated Christian teacher of blind children in New York City and a friend of President Lincoln. Early in the Civil War, he invited Mrs. Howe, a noted reformer, to join a group of people he was taking on a visit to the site of a recent battle. Mrs. Howe accepted the invitation. On the trip, she heard many Union soldiers singing around the campfire, but one song moved her deeply. It was about John Brown, the slavery abolitionist who was hanged for his part in the famous Harpers Ferry raid. When Mrs. Howe returned to Washington, she couldn't get the tune she had heard out of her mind and its haunting melody stirred her to compose new words for it — words which reflected her faith in those trying days. In a Washington hotel room, she wrote the hymn which was to become the marching song of an Army, and in years to come a testimony of faith for a nation.

Mine eyes have seen the glory of the coming of the Lord;
He is trampling out the vintage where the grapes of wrath are stored;
He hath loosed the fateful lightning of His terrible swift sword;
His truth is marching on.

Glory! glory, hallelujah!
Glory! glory, hallelujah!
Glory! glory, hallelujah!
Our God is marching on.

Easter is another one of those special occasions which calls for prayerful song selection. One of my favorite Easter solos is "Were You There?" and I've sung it in some memorable sunrise services — at Soldier Field in Chicago and in the Rose Bowl, each before audiences in the tens of thousands.

But the time I cherish most is just before this last Easter when I was in Jerusalem at the Garden Tomb in the Gordon's Calvary area. The keeper of the tomb, a young man who was converted at our Amsterdam Crusade a few years ago, asked me to sing "Were You There?" for the group touring that historic site. I did as he asked concluding with a different ending from that which was written.

Though not original with me, I think the last stanza should be more triumphant than that in the books. So instead of singing:

Were you there when they laid him in the tomb?

I sing:

> **Were you there when He rose up from the dead?**
> **Were you there when He rose up from the dead?**
> **Sometimes I feel like shouting "Glory, glory, glory."**
> **Were you there when He rose up from the dead?**

That sentiment more accurately states my feelings about Christ's victory over death.

5

Songs That Lift the Heart

A few years ago I did an album entitled *Hymns That Have Lived 100 Years*. It included such numbers as "Rock of Ages," "Fairest Lord Jesus," "Nearer My God To Thee," and "Abide With Me." Of course, many hymns we sing today are over 100 years old. Age neither dims their truth or beauty nor does it lessen the impact of some of the legends that have followed these hymns through their decades of popularity.

Singing "Jesus, Lover of My Soul" recently, I was reminded of a story Ira D. Sankey told about that Charles Wesley composition. One afternoon on a Hudson River liner out of New York, Sankey was singing that song to a gathering of people.

> **Jesus, lover of my soul,**
> **Let me to Thy bosom fly...**

When a man came to him excitedly out of the crowd. "Were you in the Union Army?" the man asked.

"Yes, I served in Maryland."

"Were you at such and such battle?"

"Yes."

"Could you have been singing that hymn one night while you were on sentry duty?"

"Yes, I even remember the night," Sankey told me.

"And I remember having a bead on you, but hearing you sing that great hymn I could not squeeze the trigger."

That story has a World War II parallel. It is told by a friend of mine, Burt Frizen, who lives in Wheaton, Illinois. While attending college at Wheaton, Burt distinguished himself with his fine baritone voice. But his college studies were interrupted by the war. Serving in

Germany, he was seriously wounded and lay dying for six hours. He passed in and out of consciousness, aware at each wakening that his life was ebbing faster and faster.

To face that moment, he began singing a hymn his mother had taught him.

> **There is a name to me so dear,**
> **Like sweetest music to my ear;**
> **For when my heart is troubled, filled with fear,**
> **Jesus whispers peace.**

As he sang, a German soldier came upon him, his bayonet fixed. Burt anticipated the worst but kept singing. As he sang he felt himself being lifted up. He was carried to a nearby stone ledge. There the enemy soldier left Burt unharmed. A few minutes later, he was discovered and rescued by his own medics.

Though the great hymns of the past are fine, they should not cloud our perception to recognize that some inspiring music is being written today. As I try to select contemporary numbers to sing, I often wonder which of them will be in hymn books a hundred years from now. More than a few, I suspect.

It has been my privilege to know many of the leading hymn writers and gospel musical talents of our day and they are truly an outstanding lot — well-schooled, dedicated, committed — such men as John Peterson of Grand Rapids, musical editor of the Singspiration series, published by Zondervan. One of the most prolific composers today, John does both words and music — and does them well. How many times have you sung:

> **It took a miracle to put the stars in place**
> **It took a miracle to hang the world in space**
> **But when He saved my soul, cleansed, and made me whole,**
> **It took a miracle of love and grace.**

Many times, right? Well, then you know John Peterson by music and poetry if not by face. He also has written "Shepherd of Love" and a beautiful Christmas cantata.

I first came into contact with John when he joined the staff of WMBI in the mid-forties. Few people who ever heard his sign-off program at sundown will ever forget it. (WMBI's license limits its broadcasting hours to sunset so John's program closed the day for the station.) Playing an Hawaiian guitar, his tender interpretation of the old hymns could and did bring tears to the eyes. As a matter of fact, the station still plays those tapes and his music still has the same effect on me. He was often accompanied at the organ by some other dear friends of mine — Don Hustad, John Innes and Gil Mead. All of them deserve the appreciation of gospel music lovers for the dedication of their talents to the Lord.

Gil and John live nearby and are available when I need help. Not long ago, Gil played for me in Oklahoma City at a state teachers' convention and afterward we got to talking about his hobby — building and repairing pipe organs.

"Do you ever have any pipes you don't know what to do with?" I asked him.

"Do I," he said. "Come over and I'll give you a barrelfull."

And that's just what happened. I must have transferred a hundred pipes from Gil's basement to mine. I don't know what I'm going to do with them, except maybe blow a high E once in a while. (Whenever I let go with one of those blasts from the basement, I always give Erma a start. "Boys must play," she will call down from the kitchen.)

Another dedicated Christian musician is John Innes from Scotland. He heard the Crusade from Harringay Arena in London over the old World War II telephone landlines which carried broadcasts to 500 auditoriums throughout the islands. That was a providential windfall. Had it not been for Bob Benninghoff, ABC engineer out of Chicago, John and millions of others would not have heard those services. Bob Benninghoff had remembered that during World War II landlines had been used to communicate throughout Great Britain. He contacted the post office department, found the lines to be intact and permission was received to use them during the Crusade.

John Innes was one of those who heard the broadcasts. He was a boy of sixteen then. At eighteen, he came to America. He graduated from Wheaton and received his Master's at Northwestern University.

It was during this time that the paths of Don Hustad and John Innes crossed. Speaking of Don, few people in this line of work are more respected than he is.

After many years with the Billy Graham team, he is now a full-time professor of music at Louisville's Southern Baptist Seminary. He still finds time to travel with me to an occasional evening of sacred music concert or to help out at a Crusade.

There are so many memories Don and I share about music from WMBI through some of the great Crusade meetings right up to the present. While I was working on this book, Don played at the Lexington, Kentucky, Crusade and then accompanied me on a series of concerts.

He reminds me of so many past highlights whenever we get together. For example, not long ago while playing the invitation hymn "Just As I Am" he put a tag on the end of it that sent my mind tumbling back a few years to the Copenhagen meetings. There, they sing "Just As I Am" the same as we do until the end. Then after "I come, I come" they add "Oh, Lamb of God, I come." Whereas we usually end on what we call "a third," they close on the dominant of the chord. Now whenever Don wants to remind me of those wonderful meetings in Denmark, all he must do is use the leitmotif technique and he's got me.

Others on the Billy Graham musical team, such as Tedd Smith and Cliff Barrows, have had a great influence on gospel music in our time. Tedd's talent could have certainly carried him far in the classical field, or for that matter in any direction he chose. I'm thankful he was led into the ministry of sacred music because he has been a great blessing to so many.

Recently, he composed a clever song in a modern idiom which has captivated audiences, both at home and abroad. Called "The Running Man," it tells in ballad form the story of a man who ran scared all his life until he met Jesus. Finally, his running over, Tedd tells about the man's new peace as he plays "I Know That My Redeemer Liveth."

"The Running Man" draws praise whenever Tedd presents it. With the exception of Cliff and me, Tedd has been on the BGEA musical team longer than anyone, and his friendship and support have provided constant joy in my work.

Cliff's talents know no limit — neither does his enthusiasm for singing the Gospel. He, probably more than anyone else, has helped relax me on the platform and I've always needed a little help in this department. No one can do his best if he's tense, and Cliff's sincerity, warmth, grace, and sense of humor have given the Crusades a wonderful informal flavor. I'll never forget the night in San Francisco's Cow Palace in front of a full house when I forgot the words to "Make the Courts of Heaven Ring." Tedd, who sometimes may not know what I'm going to sing until I go to the mike, was given the signal: two fingers down; meaning two flats, and I began:

> **"Holy, holy" is what the angels sing,**
> **And I expect to help them**
> **Make the courts of heaven ring....**

All at once my mind went blank. Tedd began the second verse without me.

"Cliff," I said, turning around, "I guess you'll have to help. Mother told me this would happen someday, but I never figured it would happen at the Cow Palace."

The crowd broke into a big round of applause and I picked up the music at the chorus.

When it was over, Cliff had some funny line which brought another laugh and the service proceeded. One other thing: After that I started carrying a copy of the words in my little black book just in case!

Still, of all Cliff's talents, preaching, singing, song leading, acting (I thought he did a great job in the film *His Land,* as did our friend Cliff Richard), his genius is not more in evidence than when he is rehearsing and honing a choir. Inside a few minutes, he can take thousands of strangers and blend their voices into a symphony of ear-pleasing and soul-stirring music. He's the Robert Shaw of our field — no question about it.

Speaking of the film *His Land* brings to mind the name of Ralph Carmichael again. He composed the musical score for this picture which includes the beautiful "The New 23rd," which I recorded recently. All told, Ralph has written in the neighborhood of seventy-five motion picture scores and he has done all the music for the BGEA's World Wide Picture productions. In addition, he has written a great many things for TV, and a list of great songs that make one wonder how he has time to sleep.

A contributor to both secular and sacred music, the California-based composer can swing from music for Roger Williams, the King Family, Jack Jones, or Peggy Lee to gospel music without missing a note. The son of a minister, Ralph admits to liking sacred music best and his writing in this category has thrilled millions. I've done several of his numbers, and all of them are what my old singing coach, Emerson Williams, would call "heart songs." Among Ralph's songs are: "He's Everything to Me," "All My Life" and "The Saviour Is Waiting." One of my favorites to come from Ralph's pen is "I Found What I Wanted." The words are only matched by the music for beauty:

> **I found what I wanted**
> **When I found the Lord,**
> **I found more than pleasures**
> **Of earth could afford,**

> **I knew the moment I knelt**
> **How rich my life really could be,**
> **Yes, God did this for me.**

I first worked with Ralph at a recording session in 1959 when he arranged and conducted the album, "The Love of God," but my friendship with him dates several years earlier than that when he was arranging and conducting for Christian films. There is always something distinctively original about anything Ralph touches. His music is lilting, happy, inspiring.

Another exciting composer today is Cindy Walker who can and does write both religious and popular music. I first met Cindy in 1951 during the Hollywood Crusade. We were invited out to the home of Y. P. Freeman, then vice-president of Paramount. Billy spoke to the guests, about sixty people as I recall, and he invited them to accept Christ. Several people made commitments and one of them was Cindy. Several days later she wrote what the experience meant to her:

> **Oh, how sweet it is to know:**
> **Jesus loves me,**
> **That wherever I may go:**
> **Jesus loves me,**
> **In His love each day I'm growing,**
> **With the glory just of knowing**
> **Jesus loves me.**
>
> **On the cross in deep distress He set me free**
> **Greater love hath none than this:**
> **He died for me,**
> **So, oh grave, where is thy power,**
> **He's my strength, my shining tower,**
> **Star of sorrow's darkest hour,**
> **Jesus loves me.**

I've recorded that number along with many others of Cindy's, who has more than 400 copyrighted songs. Among her religious gems I like: "A Child of the King," "Tender Farewell," "O Gentle Shepherd," and "Beloved Enemy."

Her pop successes include: "You Don't Know Me," "In the Misty Moonlight," "Dream Baby," "Distant Drums."

A Texan who spends half her time in the Lone Star State and half the year in Nashville, she comes from a musical family. Her grandfather, F. L. Eiland, wrote "Hold to God's Unchanging Hand" and her mother, affectionately known as Mama to people in the recording business, is an accomplished pianist. But Cindy's story is a modern fairy tale. As a young girl of seventeen, living in California, she hand-carried her first composition into the offices of Bing Crosby and handed it to him. It was entitled "Lone Star Trail." Bing liked it and used it in his next picture. Since then Eddy Arnold, Perry Como, Jim Reeves, Andy Williams, Glenn Campbell — the list goes on and on — have recorded Cindy Walker-written songs and with great results.

Of course, Cindy can and does sing occasionally. And she does it well.

Speaking of her vocal ability makes me aware that I have written a great deal about composers and gospel instrumentalists, but have said little about some of the talented people who sing the lyrics. If I get started, however, I don't know where I'll stop. In particular, I'd single out some of the people who have come forward to lend their talents during Crusades — Ethel Waters, Lawrence Welk star Norma Zimmer, Myrtle Hall of Greenville, South Carolina, Anita Bryant — I'm going to stop! There are many who could be named.

I cannot go on without telling you a personal experience my wife Erma and I had recently with Ethel Waters, our dear friend. As many know, she sings with us several times a year now, thrilling audiences with such great ones as "His Eye Is on the Sparrow" and "Oh, How I Love Jesus." Ethel is a sterling example of what I mean when I say that you can tell a person's commitment by the conviction in his voice. She means what she sings.

Many will recall, Ethel came to us during the 1957 Crusade in New York. One night she showed up and sang in the choir. The next night she came back and, before that Crusade was over, she was giving her message in song to those vast crowds which packed Madison Square Garden.

Not long ago, she was in Chicago to star in the revival of the Broadway musical, "Member of the Wedding." As you can guess, she was a four-bell hit. Before returning to the Coast, she came out and spent her last night in our home. How we all enjoyed her visit.

After dinner, we sat and talked and I got to fiddling around at the piano. Ethel got to singing and I couldn't resist turning on my recorder. Among other things I taped her singing something that I want to keep always. It went like this:

> **Since Christ my soul from sin set free,**
> **This world has been a heaven to me,**
> **And mid life's sorrows and its woe,**
> **'Tis heaven my Saviour here to know.**

> *O Hallelujah, yes 'tis heaven,*
> *'Tis heaven to know my sin's forgiven.*
> *On land or sea or in the air,*
> *Where Jesus is, 'tis heaven there.*

When she finished Erma and I had tears in our eyes and were nearly speechless. Beautiful!

Cliff Barrows recently told me a story that I like:

While completing a World Wide film in Los Angeles which featured Ethel, Cliff visited the venerable performer in her fifteenth-floor apartment. It was a short time after that severe earthquake.

"How did you get along during the big shake, Ethel?" Cliff asked.

"When I woke up, the ceiling was going every which way," she told him. "I said, 'Whatever You have in mind with me is all right. You've got my address and I've got Yours.'"

There are many more people with a God-given talent who are writing fine gospel music today. Some of them have yet to be heard from by the general public. But down through history there have always been the Josef Mohrs waiting in the shadows, ready to bring us a "Silent Night."

For example, there's Lee Fischer, good friend and team member of the BGEA. Though many have heard and sung his musical compositions (such as "The Christ of Every Crisis" which was featured in the film, *For Pete's Sake!*), I feel certain we will be hearing much more from Lee's pen in the future. He is a man of so many talents.

There are always the inspired poets like blind Fanny Crosby, giving us new insights, new vision. (I visited the great composer's grave in Bridgeport, Connecticut, once. In the same cemetery are the impressive tombstone of P. T. Barnum, the great showman, and Tom Thumb, one of his most famous performers. Across a road where the grass was longer, I found a small stone which read simply: AUNT FANNY, FANNY J. CROSBY. SHE HATH DONE WHAT SHE COULD.)

There are always people doing God's work. People like George Bennard, who was the minister of a small Michigan church when he composed "The Old Rugged Cross." His station in life didn't keep it from becoming one of the most famous hymns of our time. The point is we can serve the Lord wherever we are.

Kitty Suffield said it best when she wrote:

> Does the place you're called to labor seem so small and little
> known? Little is much when God is in it....

When I look back on my life, I still find it hard to believe that God
could have chosen me for the work He has. I still ask: Why me, God?

To think that I almost blew the whole thing when I was just getting
started in New York. In *Then Sings My Soul,* I told about my opportunity to perform with a group of singers who were the Fred Warings
of that time. It was a fine ensemble with a good reputation, and I was
honored to be asked. It was a tremendous decision at that time, and I
was torn in several directions. Fortunately, I didn't have to make that
decision by myself. The Lord helped me and I said no. Though it
caused me no little pain for several months (the uncertainty that I had
made the right decision kept me uptight), there soon came another
opportunity in a Christian ministry and I knew for sure that this was
my call. My slot. My special place. What a great feeling to know you
are where God wants you.

My dad was a contented man because he had this assurance; so was
my grandfather George Whitney. Both were ministers. I got to thinking about these two men recently on my last birthday. I remember
when I was growing up that people over forty were over the hill —
my, they were in rocking chairs! Funny, now that number doesn't
seem nearly so old. I still take the stairs two steps at a time.

When I say that music — gospel music — is in my blood, I can support it with evidence. Grandfather George whose ministry finished in
Merengo, Iowa, in a small country church, was a lover of gospel
music.

He was slowed by heart trouble in the last years and his activities
were greatly restricted, much to his displeasure, I'm told. One day
when the doctor came to see him, Grandpa George was singing some
hymn at the top of his lungs.

"George, take it easy," the doctor advised. "Your heart can't take
that."

"You mean I can't even sing a hymn?" he asked.

"Not if you're going to stick around."

Grandpa quit singing — until the doctor's buggy was out of view.
Then, he continued. He could no more constrain his passion for the
hymns than he could for breathing. He lived for some time with his
health problem, but he praised God every day in song. And when the
end came, he parted this life in song. According to Mother, he died
with one of the all-time favorites on his lips:

When I walk in the pathway of duty,
When I rest at the close of the day,
I know there are joys that await me,
When I've gone the last mile of the way.

Dad loved the hymns, too. The last time I visited him in Syracuse, just before he died, he asked me to sing. A man by the name of John Wadell was one of his favorite vocalists when he first went into the ministry and Mr. Wadell's "theme" song was "Saved, Saved."

At our last meeting in Syracuse, Dad — dressed in a robe that hung loosely about his thin body — said, "Go to the piano, I want to sing, Son." I did as he asked.

"What would you like me to play, Dad?"

"Saved, Saved," he said, a smile coming to his wan face. He began to sing.

From over the ocean there comes to me,
The message of Christ who has died on the tree,
It tells of His great love, and His tender care,
It tells of the home prepared over there.

Together, we sang the chorus:

Saved, saved by the lamb that was slain,
Saved, from the guilt and cleansed of its stain,
Saved, saved by the lamb that was slain,
Saved from the guilt and cleansed of its stain.

That's the message I've been singing for all these years, and it's the message I intend to continue sharing as long as God gives me breath. As long as there are people who haven't heard the Good News, I'll continue to tell them why there's a song in my heart.

Singing I go along life's road,
Praising the Lord, praising the Lord,
Singing I go along life's road,
For Jesus has lifted my load.

Above: Mom Shea and her brood, left to right—Pauline (Mrs. Earl Lusk), who though widowed, keeps busy at Houghton College; Dr. J. Whitney Shea, professor of sociology at Houghton College; Mary (Mrs. Harvey N. Robinson), wife of a Wesleyan Methodist pastor, Olean, New York; Beverly, it's best we don't get into what happened to him; the Reverend Alton J. Shea, pastor of the Wesleyan Methodist Church, Wellsville, New York; Lois (Mrs. Kenneth W. Wright), wife of a doctor—a lung specialist—Syracuse, New York; Ruth (Mrs. Edward Willett) whose husband is professor of economics at Houghton College; Grace (Mrs. Bill Baker) whose husband is with General Electric in Syracuse. *Left:* The Reverend and Mrs. A. J. Shea—Mom and Dad. *Left, below:* Mother and I at the Bell piano.

A recent picture of the George Beverly Sheas at home—my
loves Lainie, Erma and Ron.

Sept. 30. 1975

THEN
SINGS MY
SOUL

GEORGE BEVERLY SHEA

with Fred Bauer

CRUSADE EDITION

Published by

World Wide Publications

1313 Hennepin Avenue

Minneapolis, Minnesota 55403

Acknowledgment is made to the following publishers for quotations appearing in this book:

From *Thou Light of Light* by J. Thurston Noé, used by permission of G. Schirmer, Inc.

From "The Love of God" by Frederick M. Lehman, used by permission of Nazarene Publishing House, © 1917, renewed 1945 by Nazarene Publishing House.

From *Moody* by J. C. Pollock, used by permission of The Macmillan Company, © 1963.

From "The Road Not Taken" from *Complete Poems of Robert Frost*. Copyright 1916 by Holt, Rinehart and Winston, Inc. Copyright 1944 by Robert Frost. Reprinted by permission of Holt, Rinehart and Winston, Inc.

From "Chicago" from *Chicago Poems* by Carl Sandburg. Copyright 1916 by Holt, Rinehart and Winston, Inc. Copyright 1944 by Carl Sandburg. Reprinted by permission of Holt, Rinehart and Winston, Inc.

From "I'd Rather Have Jesus." Copyright 1967, Chancel Music, Inc. Used by permission.

From "It Is No Secret" by Stuart Hamblen. © Copyright 1950 by Duchess Music Corporation. Used by permission. All rights reserved.

From "How Great Thou Art" by Stuart K. Hine. © Copyright 1955 Manna Music, Inc.

Table of Contents

Foreword

The first time someone asked me to write a book I laughed.

The next time I laughed again — though not as self-consciously. Finally, when I saw that people weren't kidding, I quit being amused and considered the idea more seriously. Even after convincing myself that I would like to put some thoughts down on paper, I was only too aware that writing is not my forte. Though I am out of the Blarney Stone tradition, no one has ever used "loquacious" as an adjective in front of my name. Maybe awareness of my communicative shortcomings has been heightened by close association with so many gifted wordsmiths — those cut out of the Billy Graham, Grady Wilson, Cliff Barrows cloth. Is it any wonder I have chosen to stick to singing!

Then a couple of years ago I met Fred Bauer, at that time Managing Editor of *Guideposts* magazine. Fred worked with me on an article which quite effectively related some of my most meaningful experiences and, for one of the few times in my life, I felt good about a written work. So pleased, in fact, that the next time a publisher asked me about a book, I answered that I might consider it if Fred were available to help me. This he consented to do, and the pages which follow are the result of our mutual effort.

Still, I want to make it clear that everything herein is mine. I insist on taking the blame. The story, homely though it may be, is mine. So are any errors. I've got a great forgetter and it is inconceivable to think that it might not show up somewhere in this account.

Yet the writing of this book was not the struggle I expected, but rather a rewarding, enjoyable venture. What a wonderful experience, reflecting on the Christlike people who have been so kind and helpful to me. Without them, there would be no story to tell.

This script does not, however, begin to do justice to all of the folks who have played significant roles in my life. I regret that space does not permit me to name more of them, but had I tried, this work probably would have turned into a facsimile of a phone directory — and that isn't what the publisher had in mind.

One final note: The purpose of this book is to glorify the name of Christ and none other. I pray that you receive the same spiritual blessing in reading this story that I have had in writing it.

George Beverly Shea

Psa 28:7

Introduction

Long before I met George Beverly Shea I had heard about him. I took my best girl, who is now my wife, to a concert to hear John Charles Thomas. Someone whispered to me that the tall, handsome man sitting three rows in front was George Beverly Shea, the well-known radio singer. I was tremendously impressed and spent about as much time watching him as I did listening to John Charles Thomas. From that moment on I determined to meet and know Mr. Shea personally someday. My chance came eighteen months later when I became pastor of a small suburban church near Chicago and was asked to take a late Sunday night religious program called *Songs in the Night*. I determined to get George Beverly Shea as my singer. This was like reaching for the moon but, after a great deal of prayer, I went in fear and trembling to ask if he would come and sing — at least on the opening program. After a little persuasion he came. We have been colleagues in evangelism ever since that Spring day in 1944.

The thing that impressed me most about Bev from the very beginning of our long association, was the life he lived behind the scenes. His humility was genuine. His walk with God was sincere. He really meant what he sang!

I have seen Bev under pressure time after time. I have watched him in almost every conceivable circumstance — from the battlefields of Vietnam to the largest stadiums in the world. He always remains calm, unruffled and devotional.

One of the characteristics that makes Bev Shea unique as a singer is that he sings a sermon. Many other singers are more spectacular, but he is in a class by himself when it comes to worshipful singing. In the early days of our relationship, before Cliff Barrows joined us, people would come to hear Bev Shea sing, and I had an opportunity to preach to the crowds that came to hear him. It has been a thrill and a joy to watch Bev, Cliff Barrows, Tedd Smith, Don Hustad and the other musicians on our team work in such close spiritual harmony. During the last two or three generations, scores of evangelists have had their ministry crippled by disunity on the musical team. But when we step out on that platform, in our Crusades, we are united in heart and purpose. It has been the Lord's doing and it is marvelous in our eyes.

More than almost anyone else on our team, Bev Shea has had things happen to him. He is not exactly accident prone as much as he is "humorous-incident" prone. I guess it must have started years ago. I recall he once told me of an incident that occurred in his school days at Houghton College. He was singing in a quartet, which sang at the funeral service of a missionary statesman, in his Wesleyan

Methodist denomination. After the memorial service, the funeral procession proceeded several miles to the place of interment, where the quartet was to sing again. After the service, Bev was anxious to get back to the college to see his girl friend Erma, but the cars were loaded and his only alternative was to ride in the back of the hearse. One of the other members of the quartet was on a like mission and joined Bev in the rear compartment. Since this "impossible mission" occurred in the dead of winter, the kind mortician offered to provide some soft hay for warmth. In downtown Jamestown, New York, Bev sat up and put his pale, wan face to the window. A man on the street caught a glimpse of Bev's animated face and that man's eyes went wide and wild!

Bev is still making rapid trips home to Erma.

A more recent example occurred when we were in Australia in the early part of 1968. Bev came to my room looking very sad. He said he had just had a cable from the office in America telling him that his wife had fallen through the back-porch railing. The wire said the X rays proved that she had not broken any bones. I asked him who had built the weak railing that his wife had fallen through. "I did," he replied. I related that story to the 52,000 people who were in the Sydney Showgrounds, and they roared with laughter. Although the joke was on him, Bev laughed as heartily as the crowd.

One time years ago, I was tired after a service and we had to travel about a hundred miles in dense rain. I asked Bev if he would mind driving the car. After giving him the directions I got in the back seat to rest. Seven or eight miles farther on, we stopped at a red light that seemed unfamiliar to me. I got up and suddenly realized we had gone in the opposite direction. Bev has laughed many times as I have used this incident as an illustration of how a person can be sincere, yet wrong.

Through all of this nearly quarter-of-a-century association our friendship has grown. His ministry of song has circled the globe. His singing is heard on radio and television and recordings all over the world. We receive reports constantly of people whose lives have been changed through the sermons in song that Bev sings.

It is my prayer that *Then Sings My Soul* will be an inspiration and blessing to thousands of people who have an opportunity to glimpse the *real* George Beverly Shea, whom I have known and loved so long.

                                                                Billy Graham

I shall be telling this with a sigh
Somewhere ages and ages hence:
Two roads diverged in a wood, and I —
I took the one less traveled by,
And that has made all the difference.
— *The Road Not Taken,* Robert Frost

1

The Big Break I Didn't Take

Every story has a turning point and I suppose mine came about 1936 in New York City. I was twenty-seven at the time, still searching for an area of service.

Born the son of a Wesleyan Methodist minister in Winchester, Ontario, Canada, I came to New York when Dad accepted a call to Jersey City's First Wesleyan Methodist Church, just across the Hudson from Manhattan.

I went to work as a medical secretary at the Mutual Life Insurance Company and for nine years it was my nine-to-four job. Before and after work, however, I exercised my greatest love, singing. In the mornings many of those years, I sang on Jersey City Station WKBO. The program was aired from seven to seven-thirty. How well I can remember spilling out of bed at five-thirty, going over to the church and warming up my tonsils at the organ before grabbing a Bergen Avenue bus to the studio in time for the theme song. After the program, I took the tube or ferry from Journal Square to the MONY offices on Nassau, near Wall Street. Following work, I usually had voice lessons or practiced alone. In addition to being a soloist at Dad's church, I sang occasionally at Calvary Baptist Church where my coach, Price Boone, was a featured soloist. Then too I filled in a bass part one night a week and every Sunday on Erling C. Olsen's popular program *Meditations in the Psalms* over Station WMCA.

All of this singing was done as an avocation. I was not a professional and doubted that I ever would be, for few people were making a living in the religious music field and it looked as if I might spend my life in the insurance business. Not that this bothered me. I enjoyed

what I was doing and was quite happy to be able to sing a la carte. It was an opportunity to serve the Lord and I accepted my station as His will for me at that time.

Some years earlier I had vowed to let God open the doors and not get in His way, impatiently running ahead trying every doorknob in sight. I reasoned, and still do, that if God had some new direction in mind He would speak to me about it — if I made it a point to listen. It is a principle I have employed throughout life.

Erma and I had been married a couple of years when my "turning point" opportunity came. I was making $34.50 a week.

The incident began one spring day shortly before lunch. A singing pal of mine (I shall call Tom) phoned the office, his voice full of excitement, "Hey, Bev, did you hear that Lynn Murray is holding auditions this afternoon at CBS?"

I told him I hadn't heard.

"Well, I'm going to try out. Why not come along and sing something?"

I said I would think about it and possibly meet him there. The Lynn Murray Singers were the Fred Waring group of that day, and it was indeed a real opportunity.

"Is this something I should do, Lord?" I prayed silently at my desk. Sensing no negative feelings, I decided to go to the audition. Fortunately, I had some music along so the only thing I had to do was to get off work early. That arranged, I hurried over to CBS.

Emerson Williams, another person who coached me, had advised me not long before to "sing the heart songs. . . ." "Swanee River" and "Down to the River" were a couple of warm numbers in which I could immerse myself.

While waiting my turn I learned that the job paid $75 a week, more than double what I was making. Furthermore, it offered national radio exposure on CBS. By the time my number came up, Mr. Murray had listened to about twenty singers and all of them had received polite attention, but not much more than a "Thank you. Next. . . ." A good many of them struck me as better bass baritones than myself and I considered sneaking out a side door. But while I was searching for a convenient exit my name was called.

To say that my knees were shaking is like calling the Johnstown Flood an April shower. Yet, as often happens, once I got into the song, "Swanee River," I felt at ease. Before I finished, Mr. Murray got up out of his chair and, with face inscrutable, walked toward me. He's going to give me a dressing down for wasting his time, I thought. I was wrong.

When he got near me, he smiled and said:

"I liked that. Do you have something else for me?"

At first his words didn't make an impression. I think I went blank. Then they got through. He wanted an encore. Nervously, I went to my briefcase and pulled out a rumpled version of "Down to the River," which was really too high for my range but it had been transposed three notes lower. When I handed the scribbled-up version to the pianist he scratched and then shook his head. He couldn't read it.

While trying to explain, Mr. Murray, perhaps somewhat annoyed at the delay, came back and sat down at the piano himself. He knew the song and played it from memory.

After I had finished my second "river" number, Mr. Murray nodded approvingly and handed me a piece of music ("Song of the Vagabonds" from Rudolph Friml's *The Vagabond King),* which they were going to sing at the Texas Centennial. Included in its libretto, I discovered, was a line which made me feel uncomfortable. It read, ". . . and to hell with Burgundy." (When a boy, I would have had my mouth washed out with soap for saying "shucks" — well, not really!)

"I want you to learn this right away," Mr. Murray said. "We'll be in touch."

I took the music and wandered out of the studio in somewhat of a daze. My thoughts were all confused. I had won, but lost. Mr. Murray seemed impressed, but what if he really offered me a job? Could I take it and sing a line such as ". . . and to hell with Burgundy"? If I did, what would be the next compromise?

That night I prayed about it. I thought of the hurt I might bring to Dad and my family. Alton was studying for the ministry and Whitney was teaching at Houghton College. I also thought about the radio and church singing I had been doing and the disappointment this would bring to the people who had been helping me.

"God," I prayed, "I don't know why You have led me into this dilemma — maybe You're trying to test me. Anyway I'm not going to accept their offer if they make it. I can't think this is the way You'd have me serve You."

The next day Mr. Murray's secretary called and said, "Mr. Shea, congratulations. You are now one of the Lynn Murray Singers."

I swallowed hard and answered, "I thank you for the invitation, but have decided I won't be able to accept the job. Please thank Mr. Murray for me and tell him I appreciate his kind offer." They called back again trying to sell me on the idea, but I held firm even though greatly tempted. The next few months were filled with many dark

days. I was positive I had done the right thing yet puzzled as to why God would require me to make such a tough choice.

My friend Tom obtained the job instead and I was happy for him, because he wanted it more than anything else. However, I am not sure it was the best move for him either. It led to others like it and gradually he seemed to drift further and further away from the church. So it was a turning point for both of us.

As I look back on that day, I realize how important it was. For just a short time later a much different opportunity came my way — but I am skipping too many bases and getting out in front of the story. We'll come back to this point a little later.

Singing I go along life's road,
Praising the Lord, praising the Lord,
Singing I go along life's road,
For Jesus has lifted my load.
— William J. Kirkpatrick

2

No Winchester Cathedral

One of the earliest memories I have is that of my mother singing the verse above. Not a morning went by — not a weekday morning — but what I would be awakened by a heavy chord from the piano followed by Mother's sweet soprano voice. Few children are fortunate enough to have such a melodic alarm clock, but it set the tone of our family life, one of much harmony and love.

On Sunday mornings she had a musical meditation. This hymn began with a much quieter chord, after which she would sing:

> **Lord, in the morning Thou shalt hear**
> **My voice ascending high,**
> **To Thee will I direct my prayer,**
> **To Thee lift up mine eye.**

Her playing and singing were as much a part of the Gladstone Street parsonage in Winchester, where I was born, as the windows and doors.

My father, Adam J. Shea, and mother, Maude Mary Theodora Whitney Shea (we all had lots of fun with that long handle which, of course, she never used), were married January 1, 1900, and were blessed with eight children, the first six of whom came while Dad was serving Winchester's Wesleyan Methodist Church. It was no Winchester Cathedral, only a small, white clapboard building, but Dad was its shepherd for nearly twenty years.

I was born February 1, 1909 — the fourth child — and was preceded by Pauline, Whitney, and Mary. Probably most children feel

the same, but I cannot help thinking there was something ultra-special about the parents God gave me. Our material possessions may have been few, but whatever was lacking was more than compensated for by our parents' devotion, love, faith, and warm understanding.

As might be expected, God had first place in our family circle. Every day began with devotions led by Dad. Scripture, some application of it to our situation, and prayer was the order followed.

Dad had started out to be a teacher and taught grade school for a while before he found the Lord and was called into the ministry. The Reverend George Whitney of Prescott, Ontario, who conducted a one-man seminary, invited my father to study and "student preach" under him. When Mr. Whitney felt Dad was ready to take the pulpit, he gave him his blessing to go out on his own. Before Dad left, however, he married Mr. Whitney's daughter, Maude.

My father's first pastoral work was among men in the lumber camps of northern Ontario. For two years he accompanied John Scobie, a big, ruddy-faced Irishman, who was preaching when Dad found his way to the altar. Big John had a voice as big as his physique, and I will never forget an expression he must have used a hundred times, "I tell you it's true as sure as you're a foot high. . ."

One of Dad's favorite stories, and he had many favorites, was about Big John. While on their tours of the lumber camps, they often stayed in the homes of Christians kind enough to put them up. At one stop they always lodged with a certain family in their farm home. Not only were the people warm and friendly, but so was their big collie dog — so friendly in fact that it always slept with or near Big John.

One night John had a bad dream and got to thrashing in bed. His great weight broke the wooden slats and he fell through, landing full force on the dog, asleep beneath the bed. The pooch was so startled that he went howling through the house upsetting everything in sight including (literally) the host and hostess. Though John and Dad stayed there many times thereafter, according to my father, the dog's and Big John's friendship was damaged permanently.

Under John Scobie, Dad developed into a confident, articulate preacher, though he claimed he was once the world's worst. To make his point, Dad reported that though God more than met his needs the first year of his ministry, his total income was $4.05 and one turnip. At this point, one was supposed to ask, "One turnip?" Whereupon he would explain that after performing his first wedding, the groom — filled with great gratitude — went into the garden, picked the largest turnip there, and gave it to Dad as payment for services rendered!

Most of my early memories of Mother are interwoven with music. Watching her play our old Bell piano, which came from England

shortly after their marriage, is one of my keenest recollections. She was gifted, no question about it, and her great love for music got through to me.

She recalls the time the Reverend John Vennard was conducting evangelistic meetings at the Winchester church. (I was about five.) He stopped by one afternoon to play a couple of new hymns that were to be used in the service that night.

Mother says I listened, enraptured, watching wide-eyed from the end of the piano while Mr. Vennard's fingers glided across the keys. That night Mother says she told Dad that I had more than a casual interest in music and added, "He may have some inclination towards it."

There is a parenthetical note to this little story. The "new" hymns that were played that afternoon were entitled "The Old Rugged Cross" and "Speak, My Lord" — reason enough for even a five-year-old to be entranced, I should think.

Not long after that, Mother taught me the chords, and soon I was able to pick out simple pieces on the piano. It heightened my appreciation of music, for during offertories and special numbers I paid more attention than usual. Mother used to scold me for leaning forward during musical presentations and putting my teeth into the pew ahead. I guess I kind of got carried away — I can still taste the varnish.

I particularly enjoyed hearing the big pipe organ at the impressive brick Presbyterian church. On special occasions we would attend services there and I recall how beautiful it sounded, especially in comparison to our church's old reed organ. I couldn't understand why we didn't have a pipe organ too.

Mother explained that a pipe organ was very expensive but that maybe I'd like a mouth organ — typical of her resourcefulness. How thrilled I was when she and Dad got me one for my birthday. Soon I was down behind the barn playing "Home Sweet Home" and other harmonica classics. But what I loved most of all was taking a long deep breath and holding a chord until my face turned blue. The sound reminded me of the sonorous Presbyterian church organ. It reminded my brothers and sisters of someone in intense pain. That's why I was down behind the barn.

I liked it best down there anyway, for that is where my imaginary horse, Midnight, was tied. He was a beautiful animal, really appreciative of my playing. At least that's what he said.

When bedtime came I often took the mouth organ with me and played it under the covers. More than once, Mother says, she found

me asleep with the harmonica cupped near my lips.

Another musical memory about this time is the Saturday night town band performances. Dad would take me uptown to hear the first part of the program, and then he'd bring me home to bed by nine o'clock.

I can remember those half-mile, summer walks through the semi-darkness, holding securely to Dad's hand. The lamps at the street corners carved pale yellow tepees out of the night and seemed more effective as insect attractors than light projectors.

All the while, at our backs, the band music was fading and nature's orchestra — the crickets and locusts — became more prominent. Yet the strains of "In the Good Old Summertime," "Meet Me In St. Louis," "Wait Till the Sun Shines, Nellie," and the like filtered through and were still audible when we reached our front porch where Mother often sat waiting.

The band was playing our last night in Winchester. Earlier that year, Dad had called a family council and told us he felt led to go back on the road to preach. We were moving to Houghton, New York, where there was a fine Christian academy. There was an adult-sounding logic to the plan, but the thought of leaving Winchester broke my heart.

The last night there in the Gladstone Street parsonage, I remember passing — on the way to my room — the rows of packed cardboard boxes and the heavily crated piano. Once in bed, I heard the band playing off in the distance. I knew that it would be the last time ever — and I cried myself to sleep.

To see him striding along the profile of a
hill on a windy day, one might have
mistaken him for . . . some scarecrow eloped
from a cornfield.

— Wahington Irving's description of Ichabod Crane.

3

A Monument of Shyness

When I walked into our new house in Houghton, New York, the first thing I saw was the mangled crate, which held our prized Bell piano. Inside I could see the fine mahogany split at one end and further imagined the piano irreparably damaged. We all considered the instrument a part of the family, so we were quite upset.

But Dad, ever the optimist, put his hand on my shoulder and soothed the anxiety, assuring me it could and would be fixed. I was apprehensive, but, true to his word, he magically mended the wood, and soon the Bell was occupying a prominent place just as it had in Winchester. The surprising thing was that the piano, badly mishandled in shipment, hardly needed tuning. Once it was repaired, Mother sat down at it and began playing "Singing I Go" as beautifully as ever. When she did I knew we were home again.

Life in the pastorally beautiful Houghton community settled into a pleasant routine. Pauline and Whitney enrolled at the academy while Mary and I attended public school — at least I did until an illness. My most poignant memory of Houghton was the throat infection which kept me out of school during my third- and fourth-grade years.

Perhaps a word should be said about this strange illness which put me on the sidelines. It started innocently enough. Kind of a croupy cough. But when it persisted Mother took me to a doctor, who gasped when he looked down my throat, "I have never seen a larger, uglier, more infected set of tonsils in my life." (Not very good child psychology, but that's what he said!)

By this time the infection had spread, and I was a pretty sick boy. Even after the tonsils were removed the poison in my system lingered,

so the doctor advised rest and plenty of fresh air. My classroom became the kitchen table, my teacher, Mother.

Mother was an excellent instructor. She was filled with an inordinate amount of patience, but the raw material with which she was working was akin to a Missouri mule — both stubborn and indifferent. As long as she was in the kitchen baking bread, preparing a meal, or doing dishes, I was an attentive student. But once she went elsewhere, so did I. Often, I set out for that fresh air the doctor had prescribed. Just down the hill from our place an oil company was drilling, and I spent more time there, fascinated by the rhythmic clanging rigs, than any C-student could afford.

Also I stole away to some quiet spot with my mouth organ or the violin Dad had bought for $13. How I enjoyed pulling the bow over the strings and drawing out a chord. But for a long time I would never play the violin in front of anyone. It was a part of the private world, and I savored it.

Dad, who played the violin quite well, was pleased at my interest in the instrument, but not so pleased when he learned that I was spending more time on it than on my studies. In fact, while he was off on evangelistic trips to western Canada he often wrote, encouraging me to "mind my lessons." Dad was an off-and-on resident — home for a few weeks, then gone for a few on campaigns. His cards and letters, from such peculiar sounding places as Moose Jaw and Medicine Hat (both sites of churches he founded), were awaited with great anticipation.

Though Mother could and did discipline us occasionally, most of her responses were vocal admonitions to our better side. Unfortunately, I seemed to have a strong streak of contrariness and, more than once, Dad resorted to physical punishment.

The time I remember best concerned a transparent fib, which I refused to recant. So Dad brought his Bible to my room and read a passage before talking passionately about the wages of sin.

Finally, filled with guilt, I confessed to the fabrication and said I was sorry. Dad suggested we ask God's forgiveness. After he had finished praying I let out a big sigh, thinking the matter ended, but that was a mistake.

"Though I don't want to do this, Son," Dad said with no little tenderness, "it's what I feel I must do."

Down the steps he marched, through the house, out of the back door to the apple tree. There, he pulled out his pocket knife and cut a switch. I watched him from an upstairs window. Now the sounds of his exit reversed themselves. The back door slammed, his footsteps

echoed through the house and up the stairs. "Boom, boom, boom" came the sound of his feet on their grave mission. I expected quite a tanning. Instead he used the switch on my wrist a couple of times. It was effective punishment, however, as my memory of it must prove.

After the tonsil infection cleared and my health returned, I was able to reenroll in school, but by then I was a monument of shyness, practically uncommunicative unless it was absolutely essential that I speak. I developed a nervous twitch in my chin, which was the object of much teasing and sometimes I got physically sick when called upon to stand and recite.

One time, faced with an important exam, I got so sick to my stomach that my brother Whitney was called to take me home. Whitney, who played head of the house while Dad was away, was a very compassionate brother. How I admired him and envied his self-confidence.

In addition to having a great complex about my brainpower, I was taller than anyone my age, making it doubly tough to take cover whenever the teacher was looking for someone on whom to call. When we read "The Legend of Sleepy Hollow," I knew I was a carbon copy of that human scarecrow, Ichabod Crane. I can still remember slouching in lunch lines, shoulders dropped to minimize my height. But nothing seemed to help.

The only area in which I felt the least bit at home was music, but I was too shy to play or sing before anyone save Mother.

Meanwhile, our family had grown to seven. Alton and Lois were the last two children born in Winchester and Ruth came along while we were in Houghton. (Gracie was still to come.) After four years in Houghton, Dad was offered a pastorate at Ottawa's Sunnyside Wesleyan Methodist Church, which he accepted, and the Bell piano was crated up once again.

This time she received some extra padding.

On Richmond Hill there lived a lass
More bright than a May-day morn;
Whose smiles all other maids' surpass,
A rose without a thorn.
— *The Lass of Richmond Hill,* Leonard McNally

4

My Friend Erma

Twelve when we moved from Houghton, I lived all of my teen-age years in the capital city of Ottawa. The personal struggle to find myself and lose my yoke of self-consciousness continued. Gradually I was able to untie the tight knot that bound me, but it was a painfully slow process.

No adult ever suggested to me that I should be seen but not heard. At fifteen, I weighed 170 pounds, stood six-feet-one, and looked out at life from behind large horn-rimmed glasses. I was seldom heard, but seen — well, it seemed everybody was looking at me.

To my mind, three factors helped free me of a complex that would have robbed my life of any significant service, had it gone unchecked. First, Mother and Dad's faith in their children never wavered, and I was constantly aware of their undergirding love and prayers. Sensitive of how easily I was embarrassed, neither of them ever purposely put me in a difficult position. Nor did they dwell on my problem.

The second freeing element was my love of music which Mother nurtured. Knowing that I was able to get outside myself when singing or playing an instrument, she painstakingly laid the foundation for growth in an area that was to be my life's work.

The third liberating force was a girl named Erma.

Upon reaching high-school age, I was sent to a private, non-denominational school known as Annesley College. It has since been torn down and today a gas station occupies that site. The school's enrollment was about 100, and its curriculum put a heavier stress on spiritual values than most schools.

At Annesley I met some other boys who liked to sing, and before long we formed a quartet. Though our weaknesses probably out-

weighed our strengths, we had lots of enthusiasm and courage. There must have been a great shortage of talent around, because we soon began performing at numerous school and church functions. We were on the program the day the famous Christian and Missionary Alliance Tabernacle was dedicated. For our number we chose "Come Over Into the Land of Corn and Wine." Midway through it, there was a moving bass part which I whipped up a little too fast. Before we realized it, we got into the land of corn and wine much faster than we intended, but somehow we managed to finish together. Well, almost!

Afterward, while we were commiserating, a pretty young thing walked up to Alonzo Scharfe, first tenor of the quartet, and began talking to him. I was talking with someone else, but kept turning so I could look over his shoulder and see this most attractive gal.

In a minute, Alonzo and she disappeared, but I didn't forget. The next day at school I asked Alonzo who the girl was.

"Why that's my kid sister, Erma," he told me.

What a relief to know it wasn't his girl friend, because Alonzo was a good-looking guy and I knew I wouldn't stand a chance against him. And I wanted a chance.

The next time we sang together I looked out into the audience and there was Alonzo's sister, smiling broadly. I put a little more "oomph" into my part, especially on those showy low bass notes. When I looked in her direction the next time her face wore an even bigger smile, and I knew I just had to meet her. After that service Alonzo introduced us — and that was the beginning of something wonderful.

Before long I was carrying her books home from school regularly. She lived on Clemow Avenue, a fair trek from our Patterson Avenue home, but the extra distance was no strain.

One day in an etiquette class, Emily Post text, I looked across the classroom and caught a glimpse of this hazel-eyed vision who had come into my life. So inspired was I that I wrote a little poem which I still remember:

> Love is but one great mystery,
> A secret no man can tell,
> But the God who formed the lily
> And shaped the daffodil.
> He told us to love our parents,
> Heaven our reward shall be,
> And he ne'er forgot to mention
> The girl he made for me.

— (Copyright 1968, Chancel Music, Inc. Used by permission.)

On the bottom of the note I tagged a Scripture verse, the one from the first chapter of Genesis that says a man shall leave mother and father and cleave to his wife. Pretty nervy, huh? Then I folded it carefully, wrote her name on the outside, and passed it to my buddy across the aisle, motioning him to pass it on.

Suddenly the thought struck me that someone might shortstop the note and read it. I couldn't watch. Back to Emily Post. I riveted my eyes on the teacher, afraid to look Erma's way, but finally — after about five minutes — I took a peripheral peek in her direction. What was Erma doing? Poring over her Bible! Then she looked up and gave me a smile that made my heart do a flip. Ah, sweet mystery!

It wasn't long before I was spending some of my free time over at her house, conversing with her in the family porch swing. Her mother and father tolerated me and one day invited me to go along with them to hear the famous Cleveland Quintet which was singing in my old hometown of Winchester. Naturally I went.

So did the violin. I figured that the 35-mile trip (in the Scharfes' snazzy Graham Paige sedan) could stand a little entertainment, so I came prepared. Though I was still shy of playing in public, I wanted to impress Erma so I pulled out all the stops — or in this case, all the catgut. Resining the bow, I caressed the strings as tenderly as I knew how.

Erma, Mrs. Scharfe, and "Jascha Heifetz" sat in the back seat; Mr. Scharfe and Alonzo in the front. Before we were out of Ottawa, I had the fiddle uncased and was rendering some favorites. My captive audience was tolerant and mildly appreciative. Erma complimented me and managed a slight smile. It wasn't until some time later that I learned Erma disliked the violin — or at least when played by an amateur.

On the way home that night, I put the instrument above the back seat and left my arm conveniently draped high above Erma's shoulders, reluctant to seem forward. Then we hit a bump, and my arm fell like a fur stole around her neck. She didn't seem to object, and no one else noticed.

Ah, that golden bump in the road!

Softly and tenderly Jesus is calling,
Calling for you and for me.
See, on the portals He's waiting and watching,
Watching for you and for me.
— *Softly and Tenderly,* Will L. Thompson

5

The Long, Long Walk

It was about this time that Fred and Kitty Suffield came prominently into my life. Fred, an itinerant preacher, had found Christ under Dad's ministry and subsequently became a preacher himself. What a dynamic team Fred and his wife made. She was a beautiful woman — a talented coloratura soprano and a wonderful pianist — and, with her husband, was one day to write the great gospel classic, "God Is Still on the Throne."

Fred liked to tell the story of how the Lord sent him his wife. The train on which she was riding got caught in a tremendous snowstorm near his farm. The passengers were in danger of freezing until Fred went to their rescue and brought them all to his farm. Among his grateful guests was Kitty. They were attracted to one another and eventually married.

Because of the warm friendship between them, Dad often called upon Fred to conduct special campaigns at our church. I was always excited to learn that Fred and Kitty were coming, because they were like a favorite aunt and uncle to me.

Kitty Suffield often asked how I was doing on the piano and violin. Like Mother, she received great satisfaction out of music and found common ground with anyone else who had the same interest. A few times, the Suffields asked me to go on trips with them and I helped them — in some minor capacity.

One August we spent the entire month with them at Methodist camp meetings in Westport, Ontario. Kitty insisted I bring my violin along, and one night she actually talked me into playing it. I tried to play, and the audience tried to listen. Everyone was very gracious. However, no one suggested I was ready for Carnegie Hall.

At this same tent meeting I sang my first solo in public. Once again, Mrs. Suffield coaxed me into taking the plunge — a plunge which proved to be nearly fatal.

Before going to the platform to sing, I stood outside the tent doing a last-minute repair job on my hair. Naturally, I had no idea the entire congregation was watching a silhouette struggling with his stubborn cowlick. I combed and recombed; the smiles of the audience turned into a chorus of giggles. When I finally got my locks in place, I parted the flap and paraded into the tent — into a crescendo of laughter.

A little later — maybe still flustered — I sang "He Died of a Broken Heart," and cracked on one of the high notes. How I longed to be a magician — to make myself disappear! But Mrs. Suffield just smiled and played on.

I would like to say I had a restless sleep that night, but I don't think I got to sleep. Next morning at breakfast, I told Mr. and Mrs. Suffield that I was through singing solos. "I just don't have the voice for it," I said.

"Nonsense," said Kitty. "All we have to do is transpose it into a lower key, and you'll do fine. I heard a woman ask Mr. Suffield if you would sing it again. (I always suspected the woman was Kitty.) That woman didn't even notice the mistake. Now, this afternoon let's practice. . . ."

And so it went. Before the meetings were over, Kitty had me back in front of the congregation singing other hymns. It could be that she saved my pride from a permanent puncture for, on my return to the platform — like an airplane pilot going aloft after a mishap — I didn't crack up.

The following year, when I was eighteen, the Suffields came to Dad's church again for two weeks of special services. I was there every night, though still reluctant to sing or play before my hometown folks.

It may sound strange, but I had not yet completely committed my life to Christ. Everyone else in the family had done so, but I had not been able to go forward.

Maybe it was the dreaded journey to the altar that held me back. I had considered going forward many times, but it was a long, long walk to the front of the church. Anyway, it was at these meetings that I really came under conviction for the first time. Every night when the altar call was given, I stood with the congregation and sang the invitational hymn with such gusto that the emotion which had built up inside me like a pressure cooker was released and the trip to the front was postponed again.

My sensitive Dad knew a great war was being waged, but he never pushed me. As far as he was concerned, the decision was a matter between God and me.

The services came down to the final night with me occupying a favorite seat in the very last row. Dad was on the platform with Fred Suffield.

When Fred finished his sermon, he invited those who wanted to follow Christ to come forward. We began singing:

> **Just as I am without one plea**
> **But that Thy blood was shed for me**
> **And that Thou bidd'st me come to Thee,**
> **O Lamb of God, I come! I come!**

As we sang, Dad slipped down the side aisle and around in back of me. He put his hand on my shoulder and said, "Son, do you think tonight might be the night?"

"Yes, I do," I answered, and together we walked forward. With a beloved father by my side, the distance was much shorter than I had imagined.

Rejoice, O young man, in thy youth;
and let thy heart cheer thee. . . .
— Ecclesiastes 11:9

6

Return to Houghton

In the Fall of 1928 I entered Houghton College, returning to the town I'd loved as a boy. Though I was still not sure of what I was going to do with my life, choosing a school was an easy matter. Many of our old family friends still lived in Houghton and it was like a second home; but my principal reason was that Houghton was an academically strong Christian college, as it is today.

The fact that Erma had enrolled at Houghton that autumn did not lessen its attractiveness. Erma's brother Alonzo and Dad drove the two of us down early in September. We were both excited and full of anticipation.

Wilfred Bain, whose family was close to ours in Winchester, welcomed me. Wilfred had arranged for me to room with him, and we had some great times together.

One experience I shall never forget was Wilf's romance with Mary — whom he eventually married. They were as devoted a couple as Erma and I. The big difference was that Wilf was much more articulate about his great passion.

One night as Wilf and I were having our usual word of prayer together just before we turned out the lights, he burst into poetry about Mary. He had just returned from bidding her good-night at the girls' dorm, up the hill from our quarters, and was obviously still under her spell.

"Thanks for this evening, Lord," he began. "Thanks for Mary. . . ." There was a lengthy pause.

"She sure is wonderful, Lord." A longer pause.

"I love her so . . . ," he said in a near whisper, and once again fell silent.

I waited patiently for a minute or two and then called over from my bed, "Wilf, finish your prayer, I'm getting sleepy." He didn't answer.

When I looked up, he had disappeared. He had slipped right off the edge of his bed and was fast asleep on the floor!

(As many know, Wilfred Bain went on to a distinguished music career at North Texas State University and Indiana University.)

I received my first formal voice lesson at Houghton from Professor Herman Baker. Kind and helpful Professor Baker auditioned me for the school glee club.

"You have quite a low voice," he remarked, when he told me that I had been accepted. "I suppose you'd call it bass baritone."

I told him I had never called it anything, so "bass baritone" was all right with me. Professor Baker helped me a great deal in the areas of vocal expression and sincerity.

I guess my self-consciousness interfered with my sureness with lyrics sometimes and made it appear I had not practiced enough. Anyway, the professor told me, "Beverly, study the words and music until they become a part of your heart and soul. Only then will the audience become convinced that you really believe what you're singing."

Of course, I was just a member of the choir, not a soloist. Most of Professor Baker's time was spent with upper classmen like Hollis Stephenson, who was an outstanding vocalist. (Today, Hollis is a successful dentist in Plattsburg, New York.) How I admired Hollis' voice — especially when he sang "Remember Now Thy Creator." When I told him so, he suggested I could do as well.

"Ask Professor Baker for a copy of the music and try it, Bev," he said. I did, and the song became one of my favorites.

I also played the violin in the school orchestra. Though only passable on the instrument, Fred Mix's mother thought I was accomplished enough to give her son — also a Houghton student — lessons. I tried to beg off but her plan was too good to turn down.

If I would teach Fred what I knew about the violin, she would do my laundry! I agreed, and for every hour I spent instructing Fred, she credited me with seventy-five cents against my laundry bill. I don't know how much she allowed herself per hour for washing and ironing, but it had to be worth considerably more than my fiddling. Regardless, I got a year's free laundry. It was a Godsend because my financial situation was always a cliffhanger.

To supplement money from Mother and Dad, I did a number of odd jobs, including ditch digging. The going rate for spade work was fifty cents an hour but unfortunately few farmers could afford to hire outside help. (Historians may date the depression from 1929, but many people I knew had already got the message.) I know one thing: I suffered quite a few blisters and callouses in order to earn enough to buy Erma a birthday present that year. I ordered a beautiful "pure gold" pin from a Sears Roebuck catalog, and had Erma's name engraved on it. It cost $3.50 — seven hours worth of digging. She liked it though, so it was well worth the money. And worth the graham-cracker meals I subsisted on for a week or so thereafter.

That same month a big package arrived at the dorm from New York. It contained a used, blue serge suit from my Uncle Paul Whitney, who knew I was short of money and therefore wardrobe. The suit was in exceptionally good condition, and I was delighted. I nearly ripped the cuffs off of the trousers hurrying to put them on. Then I ran all the way to the girls' dorm.

Breathlessly, I told the dean of women, "I want to show Erma my new suit."

The dean grinned understandingly and called her. Erma saw how pleased I was and exclaimed, "It makes you look even more handsome." Strange how we remember such lines, isn't it?

All in all, it was a wonderful year — full of new experiences and new friendships. Because it was so pleasant, the note I got from Dad near the end of the year filled me with sadness:

> Dear Son,
> Mother and I have prayed about this and explored every possible avenue we know, but there just isn't enough money to consider sending you back to school in the fall. As you know, things are very rough. I guess you'll have to work a year and save enough to go back. In this regard, a friend of mine in New York, Mr. Harold Voege, who is chief clerk in the Mutual of New York Insurance Company's medical department, says he may be able to find you a place in his office.

Dad had been called to a pastorate in Jersey City, outside of New York, and it appeared that the family would leave Ottawa soon for this new assignment. I would be able to stay with them and work in New York.

It was a black day when I said good-bye to Erma, to whom I was now unofficially engaged. But I assured her it wouldn't be long before we would be together again.

If we had known how long, our parting would have been even more difficult.

I'd rather have Jesus than silver or gold,
I'd rather be His than have riches untold,
I'd rather have Jesus than houses or lands,
I'd rather be led by His nail-pierced hands
Than to be the king of a vast domain,
Or be held in sin's dread sway.
I'd rather have Jesus than anything this world affords today.
— *I'd Rather Have Jesus* — Rhea F. Miller *

7

Insurance Man

A man from another planet could not have been more perplexed by the strangeness of the land than I was by Jersey City. We had always lived close enough to the country to see open spaces where one could be alone. Now there were endless ribbons of streets filled with noisy cars and trucks — all in a hurry. Anonymous people were everywhere — people with different customs and different languages. They lived in skinny houses, sandwiched one against the other, or in crowded tenements.

Dad, Alton, and I accompanied the furniture from Ottawa in the middle of a July heat wave. Mother and the rest of the family joined us a month later, but it seemed like a year.

Late at night, lonely and depressed, I would go out on the back porch of the little parsonage to escape the oppressive humidity inside. There, I'd sit and think. Closing my eyes, I'd relive those gorgeous summer days Erma and I had spent together in Ottawa: Sunday dinners with homemade ice cream served out on a lush lawn under clouds of leafy elms; leisurely walks and talks into the cool of the evening. Even the clock moved in slow motion those days — but Ottawa seemed very far away.

In August things improved. Mother's descent upon the parsonage transformed it and us. The Bell piano, which once again survived a trip, never sounded better. We all became engrossed in the work of the church and in the people of the community. Soon the word "our" began to pop up in family conversations more and more — our church, our house, our friends, our town.

Dad worked unbelievably long hours that first year, familiarizing himself with his new charge. He was not a young man any more — he must have been fifty-six when we went to Jersey City — but he was unflagging in his dedication.

Meanwhile, I had begun my work at Mutual of New York under Harold Voege, a dear Christian man. My job was to assist the medical examiners in obtaining information that related to an applicant's health history, filling in the questions we all have to answer before our insurance is approved.

I began working at MONY just two months before the historic stock market crash. With it came the tragedies that befell many people who had been wiped out financially. One day, just as I walked out of our offices, an ambulance raced up the street to pick up a man who had jumped to his death.

Insurance is a good field in which to be drawn close to the realities of life. I was twenty-one when I took the job, and I remember how impressed I was by the life-expectancy charts. These statistics made Dad's sermons about the transience of life more impressive than ever.

The work was broadening in other ways too. It brought me into contact with some of the big names of the day — a golden day in sports, vaudeville, radio, movies. Among the people wo came into the medical department were such luminaries as Lowell Thomas, Fred Allen, Yankee great Lou Gehrig, and newspaperman Frank Gannett.

The first time I met Mr. Allen, I asked about his coast-to-coast radio program, which featured a talent show for amateurs. I told him how much I liked to sing.

"Well, my friend," said the popular comedian in his inimitable way, "you just take this business card down to my office and tell them I said to give you an audition. I wouldn't be surprised we could use you."

I did as he said. And what do you know — they accepted me! A few weeks later I sang "live" in NBC's famous 8-H studio, before 1500 people and a nationwide radio audience. I sang "Go Down Moses" on both the nine o'clock show for the East and the midnight show for the West. (In those days we had no prerecording and everything was done "live.")

I got along fine, the audience was very kind — but I didn't take the top prize. It went to a yodeler who was so nervous he was smoking two cigarettes at a time and had another two or three lit and burning in ashtrays. I won $15, however, which was by far the most money anybody had ever paid me to warble.

My work at the insurance company also brought me in touch with composer Sigmund Romberg. Somewhere I had learned that Mr. Romberg had a magnificent three-manual Skinner pipe organ for sale. Dad's church needed a better instrument, so I made arrangements to go to Mr. Romberg's with the agent who was underwriting his policy.

Graciously, Mr. Romberg ushered me into the opulent room of his penthouse apartment that housed this magnificent 1100-pipe instrument. He explained all of its intricacies.

"Let me play a little for you, young man," he said. Then, the great artist sat down and gave me a personal demonstration. When he had finished, I told him that our church's organ was very inadequate and that we needed something like his Skinner.

Mr. Romberg said he would be glad to part with it for $10,000. I gulped and blinked, unable to speak.

"Try it yourself," he said, "it's well worth the price."

Without hesitation — and the audacity of my next act causes me to blush today — I sat down and played Mr. Romberg's very own "When I Grow Too Old to Dream." He gave me a friendly pat on the back when I had finished, and the conversation turned to insurance. Though I prayed that by some miracle Mr. Romberg's organ would find its way to Dad's Jersey City church, it didn't happen.

Mother and I, who took turns playing on Sunday mornings, had to continue on the motorized reed organ, which was at least a step up from the instruments we'd had before. What bothered me most was that its wind system offered no opportunity for subtle expression. Finally, I asked Dad if I could make an alteration on it. I figured that if I could add a control to the wind supply and reduce pressure by pedal action, more tender sounds could be wrung from the ancient reeds. Dad was interested, but reluctant to let me butcher it.

"Ask Mr. Keith," he advised. Mr. Keith, one of the church fathers, was also hesitant to say yes, but I pleaded quite convincingly and he agreed — no doubt sure the church would face a big repair bill.

The next Sunday it was all set up, along with a highly polished Cadillac brake drum, hanging beneath the console. I had discovered it made a perfect E when struck with a mallet. For the offertory that day I played "Have Thine Own Way, Lord" and ended it with a delicate musical whisper. When I tapped the brake drum, after the organ died, it reverberated through the sanctuary. There was an ethereal silence, except for a quiet "Amen" from Mr. Keith, who — as we used to say in Methodist circles — was "being blessed."

That same organ was used to introduce a new gospel song shortly afterwards. Once again, Mother figures in the story. She had a habit of leaving little notes — poems, quotations, essays — around the house for her children to read. Her communiques to me were always left on the piano or on my violin case.

One Sunday morning, she placed on the piano a little poem by Mrs. Rhea F. Miller. Mother thought its message beautiful. I did, too.

Instead of practicing the hymn I had intended to play that Sunday morning in church, I turned to this poem. Melody just seemed to form around the words. When I had played and sung it through for the first time, Mother came from the kitchen where she had overheard. She wrapped both arms around my shoulders and placed her wet cheek next to mine.

In church that morning, I sang for the first time, "I'd Rather Have Jesus."

Oh love of God, how rich and pure!
How measureless and strong!
It shall forever more endure,
The saints' and angels' song.
— *The Love of God,* Frederick M. Lehman

8

"Sing the Heart Songs"

Though singing and playing in public became easier, public speaking was still my nemesis. One day, I was asked to give a short personal testimony — only fifteen minutes — at a youth rally in Fort Lee, New Jersey.

I accepted the assignment with reservations, but it did seem that a preacher's son should be able to say *something* about his faith. First I wrote out a speech that would have taken an hour to deliver. Then I cut it down to the essentials and it ran three minutes. I started over. Finally, I knew just about what I wanted to say, and I rehearsed until I knew the speech letter perfect. Each intonation, each gesticulation was practiced before a mirror. At last I was ready.

My good friend Stanley Orner drove me to Fort Lee on Sunday afternoon. On the way, I rippled through the notes, checking over various parts out of context. I seemed to know it backwards. Unfortunately, that's about the way it came out. Was I humiliated! Scheduled to speak fifteen minutes, I lasted only seven. I sat down, rather bewildered.

Driving back to Jersey City, Stanley consoled me. "I thought you made some excellent points, Bev . . . and it didn't take you long to make them . . . and your speech would have been shorter still, if you hadn't apologized so many times!"

Radio seemed better suited to me: There were never more than a few people in a studio and the audience, of course, was unseen. One early opportunity came on WKBO in Jersey City. Elmo Bateman, whose radio ministry was most effective, invited me to sing on his

morning program from seven to seven-thirty. It was a wonderful experience.

I shall never forget one of those first broadcasts. It was in the middle of a hymn when the engineer suddenly ran into the studio and signaled me to halt. He grabbed the microphone, one of those carbon mikes with circular springs, and slammed it down on the carpet. Turning it right side up, he motioned for me to carry on. Afterward he explained something about the crystals becoming congealed — we were getting distortion.

Every Saturday afternoon, Mr. Bateman had an hour-long special. Solos, duets, quartets, and a variety of instrumental numbers were featured. Often it turned into a rather bizarre free-for-all because there never seemed to be adequate rehearsal time.

One day a good friend of mine was asked — on short notice — to do a solo to replace a singer who hadn't shown up.

Midway through, my friend went after a high note and missed. His voice hit gravel. "I can't reach it, I just can't make it," he said — each word going out over the air.

As he backed away from the mike, he upset the orchestra's sleigh bells with a resounding clang. The engineer, enclosed in a little cubicle with a shuttered window, stuck his head out of the opening, like a horse looking out of a barn stall.

"What's going on out there?" he shouted. Listeners were probably asking the same question.

New York offered some excellent voice instruction and, encouraged by my radio experience, I began to take voice lessons after work. I'm glad I can't remember the name of the first man I studied under — he lived up in the west seventies — because he didn't have much to offer. I soon saw that his goals were different from mine.

"In no time at all, I'll have you reaching high F sharp," he told me confidently.

When I suggested that I was more interested in learning to work with what I had, he seemed puzzled. Later, a few notes were added to the top and bottom of my range, but it occurred easily through a correction of voice placement in the middle range. I remember that this teacher charged $10 for a twenty-minute lesson. After four lessons — better than a week's pay — I checked out.

Next I turned to Emerson Williams, a big, tall basso profundo. (Many may recall his singing on NBC with the famous Revelers Quartet.) I phoned Mr. Williams hesitantly and asked him if he could recommend a coach. He said that he worked with a number of singers himself. Would I like to "come along"?

The first time in his studio, I sang "The Love of God" for him. Afterward he said, with considerable emotion, "Young man, you should sing the heart songs. Stay with them."

I never forgot his advice, nor did I forget the excellent tips he gave me regarding voice placement. Unfortunately, the time under Mr. Williams lasted only a few months. He died suddenly of a heart attack and his host of friends were deeply saddened.

From Mr. Williams I went to Manley Price Boone, tenor soloist in the Calvary Baptist Church choir, who had a truly outstanding voice. Mr. Boone was one of the top voice instructors in the city, too, with a whole stable of big names studying regularly at his studio in the Metropolitan Opera penthouse. I got to know Price through the director of the Calvary choir, J. Thurston Noé, who had asked me to join the choir on special occasions.

(Price's story is an interesting one. He came to New York from Texas intent on a career in opera. He was on his way, when Met impressario Herbert Witherspoon took a shine to him. When Mr. Whitherspoon died, Price was left without a sponsor and he lost his big chance. He had turned to coaching instead, and had developed some of the outstanding singing talent of the day.)

The thing I remember most vividly about Price's studio was the aroma that met me when I first came in the door — vegetable beef soup. He always had a bone simmering on the stove, and before any lesson he served his pupils a cup of hot broth. It really greased up the pipes!

Price helped me considerably with diction. Not one to accept second best, he taught his people to strive for perfection. Though he was a tough taskmaster, he was warm and considerate, always. And there was that personal interest. Price continually urged me to be more forward about offering my services, and it was he who suggested that I volunteer to sing for Dr. George Palmer. When this beloved radio preacher was in New York for a week of special meetings one time, he came minus his regular soloist. (Dr. Palmer's *Morning Cheer* program was heard over WIP in Philadelphia and WMCA in New York.)

Price said, "Now, Bev, you'll be going to hear Dr. Palmer, and you should let him know of your availability." I told Price that I didn't think it appropriate, but he insisted that it was perfectly within the bounds of propriety.

I did go to hear Dr. Palmer and, afterward, went up to shake his hand. While waiting in line, I wavered back and forth, trying to decide whether or not to volunteer. One voice inside said, "Ask him" but another voice said, "No, don't push yourself, Bev."

While shaking his hand, I said: "Thank you so much for that message, Dr. Palmer. Incidentally, . . ." I began the sentence Price had sent me to deliver, but I couldn't do it. ". . . your sermon tonight was most helpful." As I walked away, an indescribable feeling swept over me, and I knew positively that the right voice had been obeyed.

Later I sang in a quartet with Price Boone on Erling C. Olsen's program, *Meditations in the Psalms,* over WHN and WMCA. Price, Hassie Mayfield, William Miller and I sang "When Morning Gilds the Sky" as our theme song. By the way, it was on this program that I first learned to know such spiritual giants as Harry Ironside, William L. Pettingill, Donald Grey Barnhouse, Wilbur M. Smith, and Will H. Houghton, who were all frequent guest speakers.

Meanwhile, Erma and I kept the postman busy, carrying letters back and forth between New York and Ottawa. We corresponded three or four times a week.

What we had hoped would be a short absence when I left Canada in 1929 stretched into five years. I managed two or three trips annually to Ottawa on the New York Central but, for the most part, letters kept the bond between us firm.

On one trip up there, Erma's parents took me to the railroad station for my return trip. While we waited for the train, I gently pulled Mr. Scharfe aside and spoke with him, man to man, "There are two things I've had a longing for in recent years — a reed organ and a wife. I have decided I can do without the organ." He chuckled, so I took this to mean he wasn't violently opposed to the addition of a son-in-law.

The next trip up, I bought Erma a small diamond ring to make our engagement official. It was still four long years before we could afford marriage, but we continued to make plans for the big event.

It didn't materialize until June 16, 1934. What a day that was!

Because God made the stars to shine,
Because God made the ivy twine,
Because God made the ocean blue,
Because God made you, that's why I love you.
— *Tell Me Why*

9

A Provocative Question

Erma's brother Alonzo, who was to serve as our best man, and I left for Sunnyside Wesleyan Methodist Church in Ottawa — Dad's former pastorate — in plenty of time for the wedding. It was only seven miles and we had allowed an hour, long enough to drive it both ways.

We had on new suits and were as spit-and-polished as a couple of Marines facing inspection. I had bought a black, double-breasted suit at Howard's in Times Square, shelling out an outlandish $17.50. To think that I could get into a size forty then!

We were zipping through the spring-fresh Canadian countryside at a racy clip when, all of a sudden, I saw Alonzo's face tighten. His hands gripped the steering wheel of his Chevy as he slowed to a stop.

"What's wrong?" I asked.

"We've got a flat," he answered.

"You're kidding!"

He wasn't.

Throwing off our coats, we flew around like characters in a Mack Sennett movie — and with good cause. Changing a tire in those days was no ten-minute operation. We had to remove the tire from the rim, put on the spare, blow it up with a pump, and mount it back on the wheel.

Rumpled and more than a little dusty, we arrived at the church about ten minutes after the time for the bride to go up the aisle. The guests were becoming restless, as were the ushers who were standing anxiously in front of the church. They grabbed us and hustled us down the main aisle. There was no back door, so, as the organist play-

ed gamely on, we marched sheepishly to an anteroom to wash, dust, and comb. Five minutes later, we reappeared to muffled giggles. But Erma and I had waited five years to get to the altar — what did fifteen minutes more matter?

Dad stood at the front of the church beside Pastors Blanchard and Telford and assisted them. Erma had never looked more attractive and, though I'd never kissed her in public before, I could hardly wait for the end of the service. Disconcertingly, the minister missed a cue and sent us up the aisle without telling me to "salute the bride," as they say in Canada.

After the reception at Mother and Dad Scharfe's farm, we honeymooned in Niagara Falls. Then we returned to Ottawa to pick up Erma's belongings and our gifts and settled down in the small studio apartment we had rented at 1275 Palisades, Fort Lee — just a thirty-minute subway ride from the MONY offices.

A few weeks later I observed my fifth year with the insurance firm. "Only forty years more till your pension," quipped one of the doctors. While I was not giving much thought to retirement then, neither was I giving any serious consideration to leaving the insurance business. I had a good job and there were opportunities to serve the Lord with heart and voice. What more could I ask?

Another young fellow who worked for a fire insurance company on John Street, just a few blocks away from MONY, looked at his life in much the same way. His name was Jack Wyrtzen, and his service took the form of preaching at youth rallies.

Jack and I had lunch together a couple of times a month to compare notes on our activities. "Boy, we had a great meeting out at Paramus last Saturday night, Bev," he would say, rubbing his hands together enthusiastically. Jack's passion for telling young people about Christ was no less exuberant then than today.

Converted while in the Army, Jack began sharing his testimony at young people's conferences in the Poconos. He carried on a concerted effort to win others to Christ, and he spoke wherever he could get an audience.

Often Jack invited me to sing at his meetings and whenever it was possible I went along, with Erma ably accompanying on the piano. I often sang the hymn "There Was a Great Calm" — one of Jack's favorites because it had a low D flat in the chorus. I could reach it, but there was always an element of suspense. Jack would start bobbing his head in time with the music whenever I approached that treacherous descent. If I didn't watch him, usually the note could be handled, but one glimpse of Jack in motion and I broke up. When that happened there was only one thing to do. Move up an octave.

Neither one of us has forgotten "There Was a Great Calm" to this day.

Erma and I were on hand for Jack's wedding. In fact, I sang a couple of numbers before the ceremony. Not only did he marry a great gal, he got a fine pianist to boot.

Singing at weddings was never a full-time job for any vocalist, but requests came along fairly often. It never bothered me to accept a small honorarium for singing at a wedding, but I remember how strange it felt the first time anyone offered me payment for church work.

I was invited to sing at a beautiful Presbyterian church in South Orange one night, appearing on the same program with Erling Olsen and Dr. Harold Lindquist. As I recall, I sang "I'd Rather Have Jesus." Afterward, the church treasurer came along and handed me $5.

"Why I — I can't accept this," I stammered.

"Well, it's our custom . . .," he began in a surprised tone.

"Well, it's not my custom," I interrupted, "and though I thank you, I must refuse." And that's how it stood.

I certainly didn't refuse it because we were in such good financial shape. The $47.50 a month rent we were paying for our Fort Lee apartment was pushing us closer and closer to budgetary disaster, in spite of Erma's excellent management. By this date, Dad had accepted a call to Willett Memorial Church in Syracuse, but Mr. and Mrs. Hopper, members of Dad's church in Jersey City, learned of our problems and invited us to live with them for a while. This haven came in the nick of time.

Meanwhile I continued to study under Price Boone and made steady progress; more opportunities presented themselves. J. Thurston Noé asked me to do two songs on his organ program, *Sundown*, each Friday. "Thou Light of Light," a composition of Mr. Noé's, was the show's theme song. I love the words . . .

The sun goes down, the evening shadows lengthen,
The western hills are rimmed with golden light,
The day is o'er, the twilight glow is fading,
A silent tide flows out into the night.
Though still and deep, the darkness cannot hide Thee.
Thou Light of Light, shine through the night to me.

I was also singing each summer — for one week of our vacation — at Pinebrook Bible Conference, and it was this regular appearance that led to my first recording. A number of people there asked if I had made any records, and I told Price Boone about their inquiries.

He suggested I talk to Jack Kapp at Decca records. Mr. Kapp said that his company was considering adding religious records to its catalog.

"We've already picked our vocalist, but I'll make you a proposition," he said. "I will produce two 78's (four hymns) for you. If you do better than the singer we have in mind, we will give you a contract. If not, you'll have to take the records on yourself."

On the appointed date, Mrs. Percy (Ruth) Crawford, who had agreed to accompany me on the organ, and I went to the Decca studios and recorded "Jesus Whispers Peace," "Lead Me Gently Home, Father," "I'd Rather Have Jesus," and "God Understands." Though the Decca contract was lost, the 500 records we originally pressed were sold and eventually 7,000 were distributed — about 6,800 more than I had expected.

After making the recordings, the Lynn Murray offer came along, which was described in the first chapter. After I said "No" to him a period of personal depression set in, lasting for several months.

I could not understand why God would put me through such an ordeal. It just didn't make sense. About all I could conclude was that He did not want me to consider singing professionally. By the time I had decided this must be true, summer vacation rolled around and we were off to Pinebrook for a week, again.

The meetings opened on Sunday night, and I had the privilege of singing in a service in which Dr. Will Houghton spoke. (After serving as minister of Calvary Baptist Church in New York, Dr. Houghton had become the president of Moody Bible Institute in Chicago.)

The next day Erma and I were out walking when we heard some one call out, "Bev." It was Dr. Houghton.

"Have you a minute?"

Erma excused herself and there, under those towering pines, we talked. I can still find the spot.

"Bev," Dr. Houghton began, intently, "I've been thinking about you and I wonder — have you ever considered Christian radio as a vocation?"

"No , sir," I told him, "I haven't."

"Well, there is a staff opening this fall at WMBI (the Moody station in Chicago) that I think you could fill."

"You're very kind," I replied, "but my radio experience has been limited to singing. I'm no announcer nor much of a talker."

"Let me do some checking. I don't have any doubts about your ability. Let's correspond about it."

And we did.

But if by a still, small voice He calls
To paths that I do not know,
I'll answer, dear Lord, with my hand in Thine,
I'll go where You want me to go.
— *I'll Go Where He Wants*, G. E. Rounsefell

10

Dear Dr. Houghton

We returned to New York that weekend, and I went back to work at the insurance company the following Monday morning. For several days all of our spare moments were spent talking about the question Dr. Houghton had raised.

Erma seemed hesitant about going to Chicago. In fact, she prayed that Dr. Houghton would not write.

"We're happy in New York, and you are receiving many opportunities to sing," she contended. "All of our relatives and friends are in the East, and we know practically no one in Chicago."

I quoted one of my favorite Scripture verses to her, one that I always turn to when faced with such a problem. "In all thy ways acknowledge Him, and He shall direct thy paths" (Proverbs 3:6).

Thursday night of that week I was late getting home because I had taken a voice lesson after work. As I entered the apartment, Erma came running out of the kitchen waving an envelope.

"It's from Dr. Houghton!" she said excitedly. "Open it. I've been dying to know what it says."

We went into the kitchen and sat down at the table. Dinner was ready, so I suggested we pray first.

"Lord, You know that we want most of all to do Your will. Whatever is in this letter, help us to make the right decision. The most important thing is that we honor You."

I opened the letter and read it partly aloud, partly to myself — giving Erma the key phrases. ". . . seriously interested in your joining us . . . need to know your approximate salary at present . . . what

you are paying in rent . . . how soon could you come to Chicago if we can work out the details? . . . write as quickly as possible."

"*Chee*-cago, here we come," Erma said with a smirk.

"Not quite yet," I said. "There are lots of unresolved questions. But say the Lord does open the way? Would moving to Chicago make you all that unhappy?"

"I guess I'll just have to find another husband in New York," she teased. Then, she gave me a kiss and asked, "Should I get the suitcases out tonight or tomorrow?"

I wrote back immediately, answering Dr. Houghton's questions. My boss, Mr. Voege, was wonderful about the offer.

"Bev," he exclaimed, "That's a tremendous opportunity. I'll pray for you."

Within a matter of days, we received another letter bearing a Moody Bible Institute return address. It contained an out-and-out invitation to sing every Sunday afternoon on Dr. Houghton's new program, *Let's Go Back to the Bible,* which was to be carried on a network of stations. If I accepted, I would be needed by September first. The WMBI staff position would not begin for six months. Meanwhile, I would be assigned to the school's promotion department.

Erma and I had set up some qualifications for our acceptance, a kind of "laying out the fleece," and all of them had been satisfied. That night I wrote Dr. Houghton, "After much prayer and meditation, Erma and I feel led to accept. . . ."

When I told Mr. Voege, he congratulated me with tears in his eyes. "We will miss you, Bev," he said, "but I am sure the Lord's hand is in this."

A couple of weeks later the whole medical department, including fifteen doctors, threw a going-away party for me. They presented me with a number of gifts, including a beautiful leather suitcase, which I really needed. A few days later I filled it with clothes and said goodbye to New York.

Erma and I had decided it would be best if I went to Chicago first, spending a month or so getting oriented and settled before she joined me, and so near the end of August, 1938, I boarded a Chicago-bound train at Grand Central Station. Because there was a few dollars difference between coach and Pullman, I chose to spend the overnight trip sitting up.

My feelings as the train moved westward were ones of great expectation, yet not in my wildest dreams could I have imagined the scope of the spiritual adventure in store.

As shadows swept across the summer landscape hurrying by the window and night ended the show, I fell back in the seat full of questions about the tomorrows ahead. But I was also reflecting on the events that had led up to this move, especially the crossroad I passed a few months before — the opportunity to sing with the Lynn Murray group.

Now it all made sense. If I had not said "No" to that offer, it would have precluded the Chicago opportunity. And I knew — beyond any doubt — that here was an area of service which God would bless.

I pulled my topcoat up tight around my shoulders, nestled down in the seat, and closed my eyes. An outer warmth came over me, matching an inner warmth — a harmony I felt with God.

Just before falling asleep I uttered the shortest prayer I think I've ever said. It was simply, "Thank You, Lord."

Hog Butcher for the World,
Tool Maker, Stacker of Wheat,
Player with Railroads. . . .
— *Chicago,* Carl Sandburg

11

This is WMBI, Chicago

Historic Moody Bible Institute has served as an invaluable training ground for thousands of people over the years and, though I went to Chicago to work for the organization's noncommercial radio station, it was no less a training ground for me. I shall be eternally grateful for this "learning while doing" experience.

Though I had no background in promotion, I spent my first six months at Moody helping to advertise the evening school, which had an enrollment of 1400. I had some good teachers. Russell T. Hitt, who is now editor of *Eternity Magazine,* was my boss, and one of his assistants was Robert Walker, now editor of *Christian Life.* Both Russ and Bob have been close friends ever since.

At the same time, I sang each week on Dr. Houghton's program, *Let's Go Back to the Bible.* Not until March, 1939, did I become a staff announcer on WMBI.

During the next five years I received the most diverse radio training anyone could hope for, eventually taking on twenty-one weekly program responsibilities. Assignments included announcing, emceeing, interviewing, newscasting, continuity writing, programming (it was my privilege to initiate the first classical record program on WMBI), administration, auditioning, and of course, singing.

Each morning at 8:15 I did a program called *Hymns from the Chapel.* "Singing I Go" was my theme.

Apparently the program had a few followers at neighboring Wheaton College — well, at least one. I remember one day in 1943 — a young man from Wheaton stopped by the studio to introduce himself. He was a tall, rather thin fellow with a shock of blond hair and a delightful smile.

"We listen to your program each morning, Mr. Shea," he said. "I really enjoy it."

"Well, I appreciate that," I replied and asked about his schooling and his plans. He told me he was a student pastor at the Christian Missionary Alliance Church in Wheaton and hoped to get into evangelistic work. After a few minutes of pleasant conversation, he departed with, "I hope to see you again, Mr. Shea."

"Sure thing," I answered. "Stop in any time. I'd like to get better acquainted. God bless."

The next time I saw the young man, the pastor of Midwest Bible Church, Torrey Johnson, had him in tow.

"Bev," Torrey said, "I'd like you to meet our speaker for tonight, Billy Graham."

When I think about Moody Bible Institute days, so many names and incidents come to mind.

I will never forget the many kindnesses of the people with whom we worked. There was Wendell P. Loveless, beloved director of WMBI, who now lives in Hawaii. He is responsible for a number of beautiful hymns, including one I use often — "The Christ of Every Road." (Dr. Will Houghton wrote the words.)

Then there was Ralph Stewart, Mr. Loveless' associate and my immediate superior, who figured in one memorable bit of WMBI horseplay — an ingredient that is a part of every radio station operation.

One day organist Herman Voss had just finished the theme song on a program and I had signed off. Then I gave the station break, "This is WMBI, Chicago."

After what normally would have been a sufficient pause, I gave a second station break, certain that the studio was off the air. The engineer, however, had not closed "the pot" and, before an open mike, I committed the cardinal sin of broadcasting. In my best imitation of Milton Cross — I purred, "This is WABC, New York."

Upstairs there was a terrible commotion. "We've got our lines crossed with New York again," the engineer called out in panic. Herman roared with laughter while I hightailed it to the coffee shop. There, bent low over a cup, I saw Ralph Stewart come in the door and head in my direction. He sidled up to me and whispered "The Federal Communications Commission just called."

"What?" I groaned in disbelief.

"If you think I'm spoofing," he replied, "go ask Wendell." For the next couple of minutes, he kept a straight face. The experience taught me a good lesson. Like an empty gun that shoots, a studio microphone should always be considered "live."

Among the host of other good friends at WMBI were Robert Parsons, Doug Fisher, George Santa, Don Sims, Dick Ross, Jay Arlan, Corny Keur. . . .

I needed Corny's help one day in evaluating a singer who had come to the studio for an audition. The girl was in her second semester at Moody, and after just a few notes it was obvious to me that she had considerable singing talent.

For sacred singing, however, her voice had a distracting sultriness. I asked her to do another song and called Corny into the engineer's room.

"This gal is great, Corny, only I'm afraid she's more suited to blues singing than to religious music."

He agreed, but after a little discussion we had an idea. When I talked to her, I said, "If you could eliminate some of the blues quality in your voice, I think we could find a spot for you." She knew at once what we were talking about. She said she had learned to sing with a band that traveled throughout Wisconsin and Iowa. She also told us how she had found Christ and made her way to Moody.

"Now I want to sing gospel hymns," she concluded.

"You will," I told her.

Three months later, her voice held only a trace of the blues and we put her on the air. It was the beginning of the singing career of Helen McAlerney (Barth), whose radio programs, records and concerts have been used to glorify God in a great way.

Another audition I remember was set up by Aunt Theresa (Worman) who had a friend "who should be playing organ for WMBI." When we heard him play one number, we knew she was right. Don Hustad was hired on the spot.

In addition to our radio work, I was called upon to do a number of weekend concerts — mostly within a hundred-mile radius of Chicago. Herman Voss usually played for me but occasionally Erma helped out. (She had studied piano at the Toronto Conservatory and at the Juilliard School of Music.)

The first concert I ever did was in an Evangelical Free Church in Rockford, Illinois. I'll never forget that program because I committed a monumental *faux pas.* A careful observer of formal concerts, having heard performances at Carnegie Hall and the Metropolitan Opera, I knew the procedure by heart.

Imagining that I assumed the presence of a John Charles Thomas, who was one of my vocal idols (later my friend and counselor), I marched stiffly onto the platform, did my group of numbers and walked off. Herman performed on the organ, and then I came back

for my final group — maintaining the "proper" social distance between performer and audience.

It was a funereal affair, except for the exit of one matronly woman who grew bored with the bore on the platform. Annoyance written all over her face, she rose from her seat near the front of the church and took her leave. I thought about her protest a great deal and finally came to the conclusion that a church is not a concert hall and should not be treated as one. Thereafter I threw away the protocol book. In the future, I welcomed the congregation at the start of every concert, trying to set a lighter or more informal tone. When it came time for an instrumental group, I took a seat and listened with the congregation. The transformation was unbelievable — in both audience and performer!

Later, when I told John Charles Thomas about the experience, he laughed. He said he's pulled some pretty "dumb stunts" himself.

"Remember, Bev," he advised, "the circumstance always indicates what is proper. You must be ever ready to adjust to the situation. It takes only a *little* common sense and sensitivity."

In the Spring of 1943, Jack Wyrtzen wrote and asked if I could join him that summer for the Word of Life meetings scheduled in the New York area. Jack had checked out of the insurance business too, and he was devoting his full time to youth evangelism. Carlton Booth, the warm and talented tenor who sang for him regularly, was moving to California, Jack explained, and he wondered if I would come East for three months.

Two major obstacles made joining Jack seem improbable. First, I would need a three-month leave of absence from the station, which was not standard operating procedure; second, I had been reclassified 1-A and was expecting a letter from the draft board.

I wrote Jack that the matter was in God's hands and I'd get in touch with him later. One obstacle disappeared when the draft board called and asked me if I thought I should be considered for a ministerial deferment. I told them "No"; I was not a minister and knew of no reason I should not serve. I was thirty-four at the time and, though they preferred younger men, others my age were being inducted and I was willing to go. Nonetheless, I was reclassified.

When permission to take a three-month leave from WMBI was granted, I wrote Jack immediately and acccepted his invitation. A few weeks later Erma and I drove East for three stimulating, unforgettable months.

Oh, how sweet it is to know
Jesus loves me,
That wherever I may go
Jesus loves me.
— *How Sweet It Is to Know,* Cindy Walker*

12

A Thirteen-Week Contract

When Jack Wyrtzen and I were young dreamers clerking near Wall Street, our plans were for the most part short range. At quickly called lunches at Nedick's, the conversation might run:

"What are you singing Friday, Bev?"

"Do we start at eight o'clock Sunday, Jack?"

"You bring the songbooks."

"What church in Hicksville?"

"The keys stick on their piano."

We were caught up in an exciting work and, as is natural for young people, we were too busy with the present to talk much about the years ahead. Though Jack was a powerful speaker then, he was still being honed. By the time Erma and I got back to New York in 1943, Jack had come of age — and how he was being used!

Young people swarmed to hear him, and they responded in great numbers when he asked them to surrender their lives to Christ. It was a great thrill for me to assist Jack with the musical part of his services.

For three months we tramped all over New Jersey, New York and Connecticut. (Besides the meetings, I was singing every Sunday morning over WHN in New York.) Finally, we reached the last date on our schedule, one hot Sunday afternoon at Alliance Place in Nyack, New York. There were people everywhere.

After finishing the last solo, I sat down under a tree and tried to listen as Jack preached, but it was all I could do to keep my eyes open. An unbelievably demanding, but rewarding, summer had come

to an end. Like a swimmer who has been washed ashore after a long buffeting by the surf, I felt totally exhausted but ecstatically happy.

I returned to WMBI in September but I couldn't get the summer's experience out of my mind. It seemed to me that Chicago was ripe for youth meetings, the likes of which Jack was holding in New York. I talked to several friends about the possibility and most of them suggested I try to sell Torrey Johnson on the idea. He was enormously popular among young people and had a large youth group at his growing Midwest Bible Church.

Lacy Hall (now Dr. Hall of Trinity Evangelical Divinity School), a student at the Institute, and I approached Torrey about conducting a youth rally, but Torrey was too busy to make any new commitments. In addition to his normal church activities, Torrey had an effective radio ministry that included a program called *Songs in the Night,* every Sunday from 10:15 — 11:00 P.M. over WCFL.

Lacy and I decided that we would badger Torrey until he said "Yes." But our persistent efforts went for naught. Torrey did suggest others who might spearhead such a program, but they sent us right back to him.

One weekend I was invited to sing at a city-wide youth rally in Kansas City. Doug Fisher was our organist and Torrey was the speaker that night. Afterwards we all climbed aboard the same train back to Chicago.

In a few minutes we headed for the club car to get a cup of coffee. The car was full of smoke, loud conversation, and a host of passengers, most of whom were feeling no pain. Even in this unlikely setting, I began a pitch for a Chicago youth rally. Torrey threw up his hands and laughed.

"Bev, you just never give up, do you?"

"Well, something inside tells me we should do this, Torrey."

Then, for the first time, we talked seriously about the possibility. I related my experiences that summer with Jack, and Torrey's enthusiasm mounted.

Rubbing his chin, he mused, "We could rent Orchestra Hall . . . you could sing . . . and I know I can get Billy Graham to speak . . . he would be a good one for a youth rally."

"And you could emcee," Doug said.

A smile of resignation came over Torrey's face.

"Okay, fellows, I'm game. With the help of God we'll do it!" In a gesture of resolution he slapped his thigh, nearly upsetting a smoking stand nearby.

A few weeks later I stood backstage at the 2900-seat Orchestra Hall on Michigan Avenue and watched young people from all over

Chicago and its environs file into the auditorium for what was called
"Chicagoland Youth For Christ." Torrey and I took turns peeking
through the curtains.

"The first gallery's full!"

"Now the second is full!"

Before we began, the auditorium was packed. What a night —
climaxed by the strength of the message delivered by Billy Graham.
From that evening sprang "Chicagoland Youth For Christ" and
Youth for Christ International, which Torrey Johnson was to head.

After my return from Jack Wyrtzen's summer campaign, I bent the
ear of Robert C. Walker pretty regularly, too. In addition to doing
publicity at Moody, Bob served on the board of Club Aluminum,
headed by Herbert J. Taylor — one of the great Christian business-
men of our time.

One day Bob told me that Club Aluminum might be interested in
sponsoring a fifteen-minute daily program of hymns over WCFL, if
they could find the right soloist. I sparked to the idea and within a
few weeks they offered me a short-term contract.

But I was faced with a full-blown dilemma! At that time, WMBI
had a policy which prohibited employees from all commercial en-
tanglements. If I accepted the offer to sing on WCFL, I would have to
resign from WMBI. The solution was simple; making the decision
wasn't. Erma and I prayed fervently, seeking God's will.

The new contract, guaranteed for only thirteen weeks, was kind of
scary. After that, if the show did not take hold, I might become
known as "Beverly Shea, former radio soloist. . . ."

In the end, Erma and I became convinced that God was pointing in
a new direction. I signed the thirteen-week contract and resigned
from WMBI. It was with mixed emotions that I left, because this
chapter in my life was a significant developmental period, without
which much that followed could never have taken place.

In June of 1944 we went on the air with the first *Club Time* show. A
fifteen-minute program, it was broadcast at 1:15 P.M., Monday
through Friday. (Erma remembers those days well — all of her spare
time was spent transposing our music into a lower key.)

For the first few weeks I spent more time in the radio station's
mailroom than some of the clerks did — I was that anxious to get the
listeners' response. My eyes didn't wear out reading letters though —
there weren't that many to read!

I did check over the *Chicago Tribune's* "Help Wanted" section —
regularly . . . Tabulator, Taxicab driver, Taxidermist's assistant,
Truck driver . . . .

13

Club Time

Slowly but steadily, the *Club Time* audience grew. The war in Europe had ceased when the show went on the air, but the curtain had yet to be drawn in the Pacific. It was a time when a troubled world was turning to God. I received many letters from people who, faced with great personal heartache and tragedy, had found strength and courage in the old hymns we featured. Requests for favorite numbers of men in service made up a good portion of our mail during this period.

A regular closing feature of our program was dedicated to servicemen. Written by Louis Paul Lehman, the song was called "God Bless Our Boys."

God bless our boys wherever they may be,
God bless our boys on land or sea,
Or in the air,
We follow with this prayer,
God bless our boys.
(Words and Music Copyright 1944, Rodeheaver Co., Owner. Used by permission.)

One of the most vivid memories is of a letter I received from a soldier who had been wounded in action. He dictated it to a nurse from his hospital bed.

In the letter he recalled hearing me sing "I'd Rather Have Jesus" at Moody Church a couple of years before. It had been instrumental in leading him and his girl friend to Christ. They had dedicated their lives to Christian service and, soon after that, they began to make plans to carry out their mutual promise.

The war interrupted their schooling, however, and their scheduled marriage. He was drafted, sent to the Pacific, and badly wounded.

"They try to give me encouragement and tell me I'm going home," he wrote, "but I have talked with God, and I know the home I'm going to is a heavenly one. This I accept, but there is one thing I'd like to ask of you, a very special favor. I haven't told my girl that I know I'm dying, nor do I intend to. But after it's all over, would you go to her and tell her how much I love her and that I hope she never forgets the promise we made to God?"

By the time I was able to get in touch with the girl, she had already received word that the young man had died. With only a small tear in her voice, she gave one of the most beautiful testimonies I have ever heard, "Christ didn't promise an easy road," she said to me, "but He did promise to walk it with us. It would have been so much fun to travel that road with Jerry, but I still don't have to walk it alone."

Club Time was renewed for another thirteen weeks and another and another. After a year, though, the sponsors came to me and told me they wanted to scrap the show.

"But it's going great," I protested.

"Hold on," they said. "We know that. It's doing so well we'd like to put it on network."

It was a golden opportunity and in September of 1945 *Club Time* was broadcast nationwide for the first time on the American Broadcasting Company network. It was carried each week for the next seven years. My job was to host the program and to sing a couple of numbers, including the favorite hymn of some famous person. We did Kate Smith's "In the Garden"; Babe Ruth's "God Is Ever Beside Me"; John Charles Thomas' "Softly and Tenderly" to name a few. Through this feature, I got to meet many celebrities who visited Chicago.

The show was loaded with talent: Don Dowd of Don McNeill fame did our announcing. Don Hustad, who by this time was head of Moody's music department, was our musical director. The choir was solid with such people as Forrest Boyd, who now covers the White House for Mutual Radio; Jack Halloran, who went on to form a famous choir of his own; Bill Cole; and many other outstanding voices.

Though the show was not carried in Syracuse, the first time I went East after *Club Time* went network, Dad told me, with tears in his eyes, "Beverly, Mr. Deeks wrote to say he heard you singing over a Los Angeles station. How wonderful that you can witness for the Lord in song all over the country."

Mother and Dad were pleased and happy with the direction my career had taken. Of course, they were proud of all their children, as we were proud of them. The Wesleyan Methodist denominational headquarters was located in Syracuse and Dad was pastoring one of their outstanding churches.

Up until 1945, I had been known as Beverly Shea. This caused some problems when *Club Time* went network.

Beverly — sometimes spelled *Beverley* — is, as you may know, a common given name for a boy in Canada and England. Mother and Dad named me after Dr. Beverly Carradine, a famous Methodist preacher and author, who spoke at special meetings in Dad's churches and stayed at our house often. On our library shelves at home stood the complete works of Dr. Carradine.

On *Club Time* we had a Scripture reading period, which was to be given by Beverly Taylor, daughter of the sponsor of the program. She had majored in speech and drama at Northwestern University and did a masterful job of reading from the Psalms. Her voice was backed beautifully by organ and choir.

After the first show the men from the advertising agency came to me and said, "You know, when Don Dowd makes the introductions, the names *Beverly Shea* and *Beverly Taylor* stand out like sore thumbs. Is that your real name?"

"I was christened George Beverly Shea," I told them, "but I've always gone by Bev or Beverly."

They asked if I would consider changing it to George Shea for the show. I hesitated — I had been on radio in Chicago since 1938 and had always been billed as Beverly. When they suggested George Beverly Shea, I thought fleetingly that John Charles Thomas might think I was imitating him, but we made the change and I have used that name ever since.

Before I appeared on *Club Time,* however, I was asked to join AFRA (American Federation of Radio Artists) — now AFTRA (the "T" for television, of course). One day I received a letter from the union, addressed to Miss Beverly Shea, informing me of a beauty contest. I was invited to compete.

"Bring your bathing suit and a smile to the Palmer House on such and such a date," the promotional piece read. I had a notion to do it because I sure needed the publicity, but I chickened out!

Club Time was an excellent break for me. Not only was it a highly successful show, it was one of quality and dignity. The additional revenue it brought into the family coffers was welcome, too. For the first time in our marriage, our budget had a little surplus.

But just about that time we suffered a setback. Erma became critically ill and was rushed to the hospital. Doctors discovered that she had pernicious anemia and ordered transfusions immediately. For two or three days we didn't know what the outcome would be. Friends rushed to our aid. Some gave blood. Others prayers. Then the tables turned; she began to recover. Our hearts were full of gratitude.

The doctors said Erma's health would return, but, "She will need lots of rest. It would be best if you could get out of the city where she could have plenty of fresh air."

We had no idea where that might be, but God knew all along.

. . . Where is God my maker, who giveth
songs in the night . . .?
— Job 35:10

14

A Visit from Billy Graham

About the time we made our debut on *Club Time* over WCFL, Torrey Johnson was trying to free himself from *his* WCFL program,
Songs in the Night.

Torrey wanted the program to continue, but his growing preaching
and teaching commitments left him little choice but to give it up. He
began to look around for a replacement and the man he turned to was
young Billy Graham — only months out of Wheaton. Billy had accepted the call of The Village Church in Western Springs, Illinois,
twenty miles southwest of Chicago. Its congregation numbered 150,
just a few more than the choir of Torrey's Midwest Bible Church.
When Torrey phoned Billy in 1943 to ask him if he would like to take
over the program, Billy was dumbfounded.

"Out of the question," he said. "There must be many others better
qualified. . . ." Torrey's rebuttal was that he had prayed about it
and felt "guided to call you."

This thought made Billy pause — "If the Lord wants me to do this
. . . ." He told Torrey he would pray about it, too, and he did —
with his young bride, Ruth.

The result of their prayers affirmed Torrey's guidance, so Billy
took the matter to his board of deacons, who met in the basement of
their church because that *was* the church. The struggling congregation had a total weekly pledge of $86.50.

Imagine Billy asking them to sponsor a radio program at a cost of
better than $100 a week! It was preposterous. What board of deacons
would have told him otherwise? Undaunted, Billy, with the vision

that was to epitomize his ministry to come, talked about such things as "opportunity, challenge, and faith." The board teeter-tottered.

"On the one hand. . . ."

"On the other hand. . . ."

Finally, Billy made a proposition. If they agreed to try it, he would do without a week's salary ($45). That broke the stalemate. The deacons capitulated and The Village Church of Western Springs was in the radio business — lock, stock, and pastor's paycheck.

In the past, the program had always featured music as well as preaching, so Billy looked around for help. That's when he drove to Chicago to see me. How he enjoys telling about that visit.

"I had to go through three secretaries," he begins. "The last one said Mr. Shea was preparing his program and could not possibly be disturbed. I turned to go, but something stopped me. Instead of walking through the door that led to the street, I walked through the door which said BEVERLY SHEA in big bold letters."

About the only thing I will vouch for in this story is the fact that they had my name on the door — in the decal letters you buy at Woolworth's, I think. Anyway, I looked up to see Billy standing in front of my desk.

I asked him to sit down, and he told me all about his venture.

"Good for you," I told him. "I know you'll do a good job. God bless you."

But Billy had not come for a blessing. Suddenly, he leaned forward and asked flatly, "Will you sing on the program and lead the choir?"

"Well, I — I — I don't know, I'm pretty busy here and . . . ." I tried to think of the long drive out to Western Springs every Sunday night, but my tongue sputtered like a jalopy with kerosene in the tank.

But before he left I had agreed to help out.

It was the beginning — the humble beginning — of an unbelievable journey.

On a Sunday evening in January, 1944, we went on the air. Billy gave quiet meditations interspersed with gospel music. Don Hustad was at the organ, the King's Carollers sang regularly and I usually did three or four solos each program.

One interesting innovation was lights that transformed the Village Church into a radio studio. They were one of my small contributions. I had placed colored floods at the front of the sanctuary to try to give it a studio effect. I had seen similar lighting used before and suggested to Billy that blue, red, and amber illumination might create an

atmosphere attractive to young people. He was enthusiastic about the idea, and the lights became a permanent part of the decor.

Billy wanted to reimburse me for the small expenditure, but I had already learned that he and Ruth had sacrificed a week's salary to get the program on the air, so I was not about to accept any more money out of his pocket.

From the start, the meetings at The Village Church in Western Springs were a great inspiration, not only to the radio audiences but to the crowds that filled the little church to hear the service "live." Young people from all over the Chicago area came to hear Billy's effective messages, and they were not disappointed.

Dynamic, hard-hitting, challenging, Billy was not just another bright young minister. He was fresh, vibrant, and filled — as certainly as anyone has ever been filled — with the Holy Spirit. On our drives back to Chicago late Sunday nights, Erma and I marveled about this young man's ministry. It was exciting to be a part of something wonderful unfolding.

Just what that something might be, we had no idea. Yet from our vantage point it was not hard to recognize that in Billy Graham God had a totally receptive vessel.

When Billy and Ruth learned that Erma's doctor had recommended a move to the country, they began to look for a home for us in Western Springs. We had only $500 in our savings account, but they searched diligently for "that perfect place."

One Saturday we drove out to look at a house they thought particularly suitable. Billy and Ruth were out behind the place, standing waist-deep in timothy hay, when we drove up.

"What do you think of this one, Bev?" Billy asked enthusiastically.

It was a fine-looking place and I told him so. "Except what am I supposed to use for cash?"

"Come on," he kidded. "You're well enough heeled to buy two or three like this."

Erma and I talked about the idea for a couple of weeks without coming to a decision. Then one day Will Ebner, an old friend from New York, phoned me. We had a long chat, and I told him we were considering a move to the suburbs because of Erma's health.

"We've been house hunting." I stopped right there. Will is one of those people who has a facility for sensing others' needs.

"That will take some cash. How are you fixed?" he asked.

"None of that," I told him. "We'll work this one out."

"Sure *we* will," he responded. And we did.

In the end, Will loaned us the $2500 needed to swing the deal.

In the spring of 1944, we packed our few belongings into the car, said good-bye to Chicago and our studio apartment at 601 Deming Place, drove to Western Springs and moved into the home where we have lived ever since.

Billy and Ruth were waiting to help us unload, but we didn't have many armloads. I think the two of them finally saw clearly our financial picture, when they saw how little furniture we had.

That evening we had dinner at the Grahams' small apartment in Hinsdale. They had been married only a year, but Ruth was already a fine cook and she had prepared a delicious meal. After dinner, the conversation turned to our mutual plans. Billy expected to be called into the service as a chaplain shortly, but his thoughts were projected far beyond military duty. He talked a lot about his after-the-war plans which were vague, of course, but all Christ-centered. Little did I dream that I would be a part of those plans.

Do it again.
Your voice has lost its sonority.
You're like a foggy day.
— Gino Monaco

15

Gino as in Genius

Billy Graham's stay in Western Springs was an abbreviated one, lasting only a year. He was commissioned a lieutenant in the Army and was awaiting orders to report for duty as a chaplain, when he came down with mumps in October of 1944. Normally, this illness would be only a slight inconvenience, but Billy's case took the most noxious form and he was flat on his back for six weeks.

At one time he became delirious and Ruth thought he was dying. When he was well enough to be up and around, I stopped by to see him. He was thin as a young birch tree and about the same color.

Though it is hard to find any pluses in such a painful experience, the delay did work to Torrey Johnson's advantage. Torrey, who was now fully engaged in laying the foundation for Youth for Christ, was unsure of his next move. He and Billy had outlined some rough plans but Billy's expected departure had temporarily eliminated him from the picture. However, while he was convalescing after the mumps, Torrey got an idea.

Billy's physical condition would surely warrant a desk job in the Chaplains' Corps, no doubt stateside. Torrey reasoned that Billy could do more for the youth of America and, indirectly, for the war effort through Youth for Christ.

Torrey reasoned with Billy but found him reluctant to resign his commission. Still, Billy knew there was truth in Torrey's words. After much prayer and personal soul-searching, he finally agreed. He was released from the Army and began the work that was to take him all over America and, in 1946, to England.

Occasionally our paths crossed and we caught up on our mutual activities. I continued on *Songs in the Night* — first with Peter Stam and then with Lloyd Fesmire, who followed Billy — and, of course, *Club Time.*

Meanwhile there was regular voice training. After leaving New York, I had looked about for a new vocal coach and had written John Charles Thomas, the opera star, for advice.

He answered with a simple directive, "Go to Gino Monaco." I had figured Mr. Thomas might have two or three recommendations, but he seemed positive that Mr. Monaco was the only one I should consider, so I went to his studio at the Fine Arts Building on South Michigan Avenue and asked him if he would give me vocal instruction.

Mr. Monaco did not exactly jump at the opportunity. He looked me over discriminatingly — much as a judge might to select best of breed at the Westminster Dog Show. Primarily, he was interested in motivation.

"Why do you want to take lessons?" he asked in a voice that had the kiss of Milano on every syllable. When I told him my reason for studying, he seemed annoyed.

"You mean you want to do all this to sing hymns? Mama mia!"

One further complication came up: Mr. Monaco liked to begin training students at about eighteen. Usually he taught them for several years, before they were allowed to perform. I was already singing in public when I came to him.

But, finally satisfied that my intentions were sound, he stroked his neatly trimmed moustache, straightened his trademark bow-tie, pulled at the sleeve of his impeccably tailored suit, and announced, "I will teach you, Mr. Shea."

Somehow I didn't expect to make it!

(Mr. Monaco's dedication to his profession, his great skill in communicating his vast knowledge of music, and his warm friendship were to become invaluable to me. And over the years, he has remained one of my dear friends.)

When I went for the first lesson, he heard me run up and down a few vocal scales, and then announced, "I can see you have been working with your breathing for a number of years. Well, you have been concentrating on it *too* much. I can tell few pupils to forget their breathing, but *you* — forget it!"

Later, he told me I was doing fine with the breath control. It was much more natural and relaxed, he said. But his greatest contribution

was in diction — diction and voice placement. Some of Gino's more memorable coaching lines were:

"Sing as you talk."

"Perfect diction will make perfect tone."

"Put the words on your breath and let them float away."

"Do it again. Your voice has lost its sonority. You're like a foggy day."

"Make your vowels liquid and limpid."

Before each lesson, as Mr. Monaco took his place at the piano, he always asked about our work. I would start to talk and he would interrupt, "You're letting your voice down in your throat. Up here. Now give me that last sentence again."

I would pick up where I had left off in the story, but soon he would break in again, "Good, good! Now *sing* that last sentence. Sing as you talk."

One day a scout for a light opera company heard the end of a lesson. Mr. Monaco told me the following week, "He liked the way you hit your low D's, and he wondered if you wanted to sing in one of his operettas. He is casting and he thought he could use you. I told him you would not be interested. Did I give him the right answer?"

"Yes, you did," I assured him.

Mr. Monaco had come to understand my musical goals, and it pleased me to hear him report this incident. He did not censure me for being foolish; instead his respect for that commitment to sacred music grew. So did our friendship.

Gino Monaco's training also helped me achieve a "vocal line" which helped eliminate voice fatigue. Coupled with the instruction received in New York, my confidence grew — at least when it came to singing. I was still no William Jennings Bryan at public speaking.

I remember writing to Dad one day, telling him that I had agreed to give a short talk. "Won't you please write out a brief outline for me? And include an anecdote or two," I begged.

Dad's reply took only a couple of lines on a penny postcard, "Son, God helped Balaam's donkey to talk, and He can do something for you. Love, Dad."

Dad's fifty-three-year ministry came to an end in 1945. He was seventy-three when all of the family gathered to hear him deliver his final sermon. It was a Sunday evening, and the church was full to overflowing. Dad was suffering from a malignancy and, too weak to stand at the pulpit, he spoke from a straightbacked, wooden chair placed — lonely-like — in the middle of the platform.

But Dad was not alone. Inspired by the Spirit, he gave a wonderful message, full of his steadfast faith and infectious love.

Less then a year later, he went to his reward in heaven. On his lap, when he fell asleep for the last time, was a notebook in which we found these words — the very last he had written:

"Life has been wonderful.
The promises of God precious.
The eternal hope glorious."

I will sing the wondrous story
  of the Christ who died for me,
Sing it with the saints in glory
  gathered by the crystal sea.
— Francis Rowley

16

The Team

In May of 1947, I received the first of two letters postmarked Montreat, North Carolina. They were from Billy Graham, who, with Cliff Barrows, had just returned from a 6-month, 27-city, 360-meeting tour of the British Isles. The meetings for Youth for Christ, which had gotten off to a rocky start, wound up with a glorious homestretch finish. Billy's spirits were ionosphere-high. He wrote:

> Bev, it was just tremendous to see the Holy Spirit work in these meetings. We went, of course, to minister to young people, but more and more parents and grandparents came along with them. There is the feeling among some of us that we should go back again some day and hold a campaign not directed primarily to youth. We have received similar requests here in the States. Right now my thoughts are turning to a three-week, city-wide rally scheduled for November in Charlotte. I have asked Cliff Barrows and my old schoolmate Grady Wilson (who was then a minister in South Carolina) to join me. I still have not asked a soloist because I wanted to discuss the matter with you. Bev, more and more your name has been on my mind and I am convinced the Lord wants you to be our soloist in these upcoming meetings. Though I know your commitments in Chicago are heavy, I trust you will pray about this matter and write me very soon.

I wrote back and told Billy I would be honored to take part in these meetings, except that I would need to fly back to Chicago each Saturday for *Club Time* and this might put more of a burden on the finance committee than would be feasible.

Within days, he answered:

> Bev, don't worry about the cost of commuting between our meetings and Chicago. I know you must honor your commitments. We shall be

happy to cover your expenses. Unless you have other reservations, I shall inform the Charlotte committee that you will be our soloist. It will be good to be together again, Bev.

In November I flew to Charlotte where Billy, Cliff, Grady, and I teamed up for the first time. Though the meetings were not limited to youth, plenty of young people, who identified Billy and Cliff with Youth for Christ, were present. It was a successful campaign from every aspect. After two weeks of packed meetings in the First Baptist Church on Tryon Street, we had to move to the Armory for the final week in order to accommodate the crowds.

The first number I did at the Charlotte meetings, which most of us consider the unofficial launching of the Crusades, was "I Will Sing the Wondrous Story." It was one of Billy's favorites. (I think I sang it on Arthur Smith's radio program, too. I met Arthur in Charlotte in 1947. A great friend, who has a special talent, his compositions "The Shadow of a Cross" and "I Saw a Man" hold a special place in my heart.)

I learned early that Billy had some songs he liked better than others, and on occasion he might ask before a service, "Bev, how about singing 'Roll, Jordan, Roll'?" In later days, he hasn't done this as much, because our lines of communication have developed to the point that I can just about guess what he would like to hear by knowing his sermon topic. The choice of the number I do, just before the message, is particularly important, and I make it a point to pray over it.

One of my most pleasant memories of the Charlotte meetings was the presence of Billy's mother and father. Billy's dad once served on the committee that brought Billy Sunday to Charlotte for extended meetings in the twenties. Mr. Graham had taken Billy, then a small boy, to hear Sunday. Now, he was watching another evangelist — his own flesh and blood. How it thrilled me to look out into the audience, when I stood up to sing, to see Mom and Pop Graham, their faces beaming.

I was surprised at the polish and maturity Billy had gained, since I had worked with him on *Songs in the Night* at The Village Church in Western Springs. Though only two years had passed, he had gained considerable confidence and poise, along with those other intangibles that come only with experience. Hearing him proclaim the Gospel authoritatively, it was hard to believe he was just twenty-eight years old.

It was also a great blessing to work with Cliff and Grady for the first time. What a contrast these two presented — even then. And

though better than twenty years have gone by, I cannot say that they have changed much. From the start, Grady's warm Southern friendliness, his imperturbability, his deep spirituality, and — perhaps his greatest asset — his unquenchable sense of humor endeared him to all of us. A great preacher in his own right, one of his other roles has always been to nip tenseness and negativism in the bud, and his well-timed wit has often saved the day. A close confidant of Billy's, Grady has been solid support, especially when the going has been toughest.

If humor is the key word to associate with Grady, then effervescence is the one for Cliff. In 1947 his gift for inspiring people to sing was already sharp as a Saracen's sword. Like Billy's preaching, which was described once as "right on the bull's-eye," so was Cliff's song-leading and choir directing. What a way Cliff has with an audience!

Billy had run into Cliff at Ben Lippen Bible Conference in North Carolina in 1945. Called in to speak on youth night, he had discovered that he had no song leader. Conference officials suggested that he use a young man from the audience, a twenty-two-year-old Californian who was on his honeymoon. Expecting the worst, Billy accepted the volunteer. To his pleasant surprise, Cliff took charge and soon had the auditorium ringing with enthusiastic song. In addition to a warm personality and a good voice, Cliff's assets also included a well-played trombone he "just happened to have along" and a talented, piano-playing wife.

"Inside of five minutes I knew I had found a prize," Billy recalls.

Whenever I hear Billy tell about finding Cliff, I think of the story of Dwight L. Moody's discovery of Ira D. Sankey — song leader and soloist. The circumstances have strong parallels.

Mr. Moody was speaking in Indianapolis before a YMCA International Convention. According to J.C. Pollock in his biography, *Moody:*

> "Moody was announced to lead an early prayer meeting at seven. Sankey, a fastidious dresser, arrived late, every hair of his handsome mutton-chop whiskers in place, and sat near the door. A windy delegate was praying. Sankey's neighbor, a Presbyterian minister from his own county, whispered, 'The singing here has been abominable. I wish you would start up something when that man stops praying, if he ever does.'
>
> "When the wind ceased, Sankey began, 'There is a Fountain Filled with Blood.' The congregation joined in, and the meeting thereafter moved with pace. The Presbyterian introduced Sankey to Moody. Moody, as his manner was, sized him up in a second.
>
> " 'Where are you from? Are you married? What is your business?'

" 'New Castle, Pennsylvania. I am married, two children. In government service, Revenue.'

" 'You will have to give that up.' "

Sankey, in telling the story later, said that when he asked why, Moody explained that he had been looking for him for eight years and that he must come to Chicago with him. It was not long before Sankey did just what Moody asked and their famous team was formed. That was in 1871 — seventy-five years before Billy and Cliff went tandem.

The only team to which I belonged at that time was about to take on a new member in Western Springs. On February 11, 1948, Erma presented me with a baby boy. What a blessing Ronnie has been. Our daughter Lainie — Daddy's charmer — was born two years later and, to repeat an old parental saw, "Things have never been quite the same since."

And Gideon said unto God, ... I
will put a fleece of wool in the
floor. . . .
— Judges 6:36,37

17

Finding Our Groove

In the early days I participated — annually — in about three "city-wide" campaigns. No longer geared strictly to young people, as in their Youth for Christ days, Billy and Cliff sought to cast a more inclusive image and "city-wide" was their chosen label. It was more a vision than a reality at first, because a good many meetings passed before we received the sponsorship of a city ministerial association. I believe the first meetings to be backed by a local clergymen's group were those held in Augusta, Georgia, in October, 1948.

Our early efforts were anything but a downhill coast. The type of evangelism that Billy was attempting had received a good many black eyes back in the twenties and thirties, and there were those who sought to discredit his ministry.

I remember well the meetings that took place in Altoona, Pennsylvania, and Modesto, California, in 1948. We were still feeling our way, trying to find the right groove. The response to these meetings was less than we had hoped for and some criticism was heard. At times a Charlie Brown-type of cloud hung over our heads.

One day Billy asked Cliff, Grady, and me to go to our rooms to meditate and pray about our problems. He asked us to list the criticisms most frequently heard.

In an hour, we reconvened and compared notes.

They were surprisingly alike. Heading all of our lists was money. The manner in which evangelistic meetings were financed — "love offerings" — was often odious, we felt. Yet how else could one make ends meet? Other criticisms for which we believed evangelists were

most often scored: anti-intellectualism, emotionalism, sensational-
ism, and poor follow-up after the meetings concluded.

We talked and prayed about some of the problems that day, which
put into focus some of the procedures that needed correcting or improving. In the years ahead, one by one, the difficulties were dealt
with.

It was a good thing that some of our early efforts did not draw any
more attention than they did for we made more than our share of
mistakes. But always there was the spirit of cooperation and team
work, undergirded by another Spirit.

Personally, I had done much more work before a radio
microphone than before an outdoor public address system, and the
change required some adjustments. Probably the most important was
learning proper mike technique. Public address systems were tricky, I
discovered. For example, the acoustics sounded excellent in an
empty afternoon auditorium, but at night with a good crowd the
system could fall off considerably. Nothing is more disconcerting
than not being heard — except not being able to hear!

Also, I found a great difference between one audio man and the
next. Some belong to the school that believes in setting the volume at
a certain level and, for the most part, leaving the speaker or singer to
his own devices.

The problem with this approach is that the sound heard on the platform and the sound heard in the audience may be widely disparate.
Other sound men like to watch voice levels closely; they crank knobs
so zealously ("overriding gain") that voices sound as if they are being
transmitted over shortwave radio.

My solution was to take a position a few inches away from the mike
and put most of my weight on the left foot, placed forward. I set my
right foot about ten inches back. By rocking back and forth, I found, I
could adjust the distance from the mike adequately without drawing
any attention to the movement. When it was necessary to come on
strong, I would draw back; when I wanted to caress a lyric, *sotto voce,*
I would move closer. Before long, sound men were remarking to me
after a service, "Man, it is no job riding gain for you. You didn't bust
the needle once." (If one speaks too loudly into a microphone, a
harsh tone results and the needle on the amplifier registers it.
Engineers call this "breaking the needle.")

After a Crusade a few years ago, a young man who sang in the choir
wrote me about my "rocking chair" stance. "I told my wife," he
wrote, " 'I now know Bev Shea's secret. I am ready for a singing
career.'

"So she sat down at the piano and I struck up that distinctive stance of yours and let go with my best A flat. Strange to say, it didn't help a bit!"

Another problem that worked against me in the early days was breath control. There is a certain amount of tension that goes with any public appearance, I'm sure. Mine, however, was a full-blown nervousness and it affected the song — at least until I got into it a few bars. Then I began a ritual used by almost everyone who performs in public. Two or three deep breaths exhaled very slowly, before one stands up to sing or speak, can work wonders for the most chronic case of nerves. This procedure, combined with a little prayer, has always worked for me.

Remembering the little sign my dad (and many others) used to keep on the speaker's side of the pulpit has also made it easier for me to forget myself. It read simply, "We would see Jesus."

I had to learn a number of do's and don'ts — many the hard way. Staying out in the sun too long has a way of drying out the voice and making it raspy. Diet, I discovered, has a bearing on the purity of tone. If I am to sing at eight o'clock, I like to take an hour's rest about four, then have a light dinner at five — steak, coffee, and half a grapefruit is ideal. After the service I may eat a little more, but it is always best to sing when one is a little hungry. I always avoid milk, ice cream, greasy foods, and cake, and chocolate, many hours before singing.

One more difficulty that needed correcting was the habit of closing my eyes. In order to concentrate on the lyrics, I often closed my eyes in public — never in a studio. One day a woman wrote and suggested I look at the audience.

"I wish you wouldn't close us out," she said. That phrase "close us out" got to me, and I decided she was right. I vowed then and there to stop, and though it was a tough habit to break, I did it. Grady Wilson says I just started getting more sleep!

On we went with the city-wide campaigns. In September of 1949, our attention turned to Los Angeles.

Billy had promised a group in California that we would come to Los Angeles for a three-week campaign. It was an annual event and this year the committee, composed mostly of laymen, had intended to follow the format and procedures they had used in the past. But Billy had some special requests. Before he accepted their invitation, he asked for a much larger tent and a budget triple the previous year's. Primarily, he wanted additional funds to advertise the meetings. At first the committee balked. Then it caught the spirit of Billy's vision

and what might have been a routine campaign turned into the greatest meetings they had ever had.

The story of the "Christ for Greater Los Angeles" Crusade has been told in detail many times before, and I can say little that would add to those magnificent days which served as a giant springboard for our young organization. It was a great spiritual experience for me.

Hundreds upon hundreds came forward to give their lives to Christ in the "Canvas Cathedral," as the huge tent pitched at Washington Boulevard and Hill Street came to be called. As the meetings reached the final nights of the three-week campaign, we were all counting our blessings. About 6,000 were coming nightly, and many were being turned away. Then the committee had an important question: should we not extend the meetings?

Billy was hesitant. He had never done so before, but promised to pray about the matter.

As Gideon had done, Billy put out a fleece, asking God for some tangible sign if He wanted the meetings to continue. His answer seemed to come in the form of Stuart Hamblen — a popular radio entertainer on the West Coast — who also sang and composed songs. How Stuart Hamblen could figure in Billy's plans was hard for most to believe. Stuart, the son of a Texas minister, apparently had little or no interest in church. He was not a likely candidate to come to tent meetings.

But because of his wife Suzy, he came and, after much personal infighting, turned his life over to Christ. Billy interpreted Stuart's conversion to be a "wet" fleece, and on the strength of this victory announced a one-week extension of the meetings. Stuart told his story over radio and newspapers repeated it. Suddenly talk of the "Canvas Cathedral" was on the lips of all of Los Angeles.

It was about this time that newspaper magnate William Randolph Hearst became interested in Billy's ministry. Soon, he was to pass along a cryptic order to his staff that was to have far-reaching effects. In newspaper jargon, it read simply, "Puff Graham."

The meetings were extended a week, two, four — all told, eight weeks. I flew back and forth from Chicago eight times, leaving Monday and flying all night on a DC-4. Getting into Chicago in the early morning hours Tuesday, I went directly to the studio and rehearsed *Club Time,* which was then being aired across the nation at 9:15 each Tuesday morning.

Afterwards, I would drive back to the old Chicago Midway Airport and head off again for L.A., arriving an hour or so before Tuesday evening's meeting. It was a hectic pace, but rewarding beyond measure.

After Stuart Hamblen's conversion came Jim Vaus'. An electronics expert, Jim had sold his talents to the underworld, and — at the time of his surrender to Christ — he was deeply enmeshed in an ingenious gambling syndicate shakedown.

"Wiretapper Vaus Hits Sawdust Trail," the headlines shouted. (Though Jim is not in the headlines today, his work among young people in New York's Hell's Kitchen merits them.)

After Jim, came Louis Zamperini. Zamperini was a long-distance running star in the 1936 Olympics. With these notables came thousands, of course, but it was the "name" converts that earned us space in the Los Angeles papers and called so much attention to the campaign.

Before the meetings closed, the Good News was front page news in papers all over the country.

It is no secret what God can do
What He's done for others,
He'll do for you. . . .
— Stuart Hamblen

18

RCA, Okay

Shortly after Stuart Hamblen committed his life to Christ, he is reported to have met movie star John Wayne on a street in Los Angeles.

Wayne inquired, "What's this I hear about you, Stuart?"

"Well, John, it's no secret what God can do," Stuart answered.

"Sounds like a song," Wayne said. The actor's nudge sent Stuart Hamblen to his piano that night where he wrote his beautiful song, "It Is No Secret."

I told him how much his conversion and subsequent witness meant to us when he called me not long after that and invited me to go with him to Philadelphia. He had been asked to speak at Convention Hall and he wanted a songster on the same program, so a few weeks later we shared the platform in a jam-packed Convention Hall.

After the program Stuart met with some of his friends, and I did not see him until breakfast the following morning. Over eggs and bacon, he told me, "Paul Barkmeyer of RCA Victor was in the audience last night, Bev. He liked your singing and wondered if you record for anyone. I said I didn't think so. You aren't under contract, are you?"

"No, I'm not," I answered. "I do have a couple of records, which are distributed by the *Singspiration* people, but I am not under contract." The thought of singing for RCA Victor was a heady one, but I didn't hear from them so I figured the matter had been dropped.

However, at our Atlanta Crusade (Willis Haymaker had by now christened our meetings Crusades) two representatives for RCA, Sam Wallace and Elmer Eades, invited me to lunch one day and advised that RCA had a recording contract for me.

"We have been commissioned to contact you," they said.

I responded that it was an honor to be considered by such a fine company, but I said, "I would want Mr. Graham's approval."

Billy's response was characteristic, "Bev, that's wonderful! What an opportunity! Why with records you'll be able to witness all over the world, night and day."

Still, I wondered what the others on the team might think, so I let the idea simmer on a back burner for nearly a month. When I was satisfied that making records would cause no disharmony, I signed a one-year contract with RCA in New York.

A few months later, in the spring of 1951, I recorded Album No. 1 with the famous Hugo Winterhalter Orchestra. My knees were banging so in the opening moments I couldn't smooth out the old voice, and we had to start over several times. Finally, with the experienced producer Stephen H. Sholes at my side, I got straightened around. It turned out to be a very satisfactory album ("Inspiration Songs," or as it came to be known at RCA — Old Faithful No. 1187). It included such numbers as "Ivory Palaces," "Known Only to Him," "Tenderly He Watches," "If You Know the Lord" (which I was privileged to introduce), and "It Is No Secret." I included the latter because 1) I liked it so much; 2) it was a way of saying thanks to Stuart Hamblen, who has since gone on to write many other songs with equally great spiritual content.

Steve Sholes gave a lot of help to me over the years. My first A&R (Artist and Repertoire) man, he served in that capacity for better than twelve years before two other great guys came along to lend me their talents. My more recent A&R's have been Brad McCuen and Darol Rice.

Steve's early encouragement and faith in me were crucial; without it I might not have hung on. The recording business is a difficult one and it takes a special stamina for getting along in it. Steve had all the needed ingredients as his ledger proves. Some of his notable recording successes were with such stars as Eddy Arnold, Chet Atkins, Elvis Presley, and Hank Snow. You can understand why I felt honored to have him working with me.

An A&R man is not only the producer in the control room, counseling while an album is being recorded, he is also an adviser in the selection of numbers and choral and orchestral accompaniment. Steve, a fine musician in his own right, was always sensitive to my tastes — as I tried to be with his tastes. It has been an edifying experience working with him and learning from him.

In the early days when I was struggling to get a foothold he was particularly supportive. I'm sure most people think that once a record has been cut, it is simply a matter of distributing copies to stores and watching them sell. Unfortunately, it is not quite that easy. My first four years were rough, because the records did not sell enough to cover expenses which are considerable. Making an album involves music publishers, arrangers, orchestrations, choral backing, etc.

At one time I was discouraged enough to quit, but Steve Sholes advised me not to lose heart and "to keep plugging." I'm glad we did, because the albums have been like a second ministry. They have over the years, directly and indirectly, brought me much satisfaction.

One highlight in my life, related to my recording work, came at the early Pittsburgh Crusade. Steve flew from New York to talk about an upcoming album and he came out to one of the meetings. Though he has always had a special place in his heart for the gospel message, Steve had never made a public declaration of his commitment to Christ.

After the service Grady found me and said, "Your friend Mr. Sholes is in the inquiry room." We went to him and joined him in prayer. It was a wonderful night for Steve of course — but it was also a very special night for me to hear my dear friend say, "Lord, count me in."

The last sentence above was intended to close this chapter. However, the untimely death of Steve Sholes this spring makes it imperative, I feel, that I add this postscript.

Early this year, I flew to New York to be a part of a testimonial luncheon arranged by the National Association of Recording Arts and Sciences, honoring Steve's twenty-five years of service to the industry. The following day I met with Steve in his office where we listened to a few numbers from my next album, the Ralph Carmichael-arranged long-playing, "Be Still My Soul." One of the selections we heard was "Safe in the Arms of Jesus." When the last note of that wonderful hymn faded away, Steve looked at me with a radiant smile and said, "Bev, those words mean so much to me — now."

That statement came back to me a few weeks later when I received the cable in Sydney, during the Australian Crusade, which told of his passing. Surely, I thought, remembering the day in his office, Steve Sholes is indeed "Safe in the Arms of Jesus."

I know not what the future holds, but
I know who holds the future.
— *Known Only to Him* — Stuart Hamblen*

19

Our Hour of Decision

By the time I had begun recording, the Billy Graham organization (eventually called Billy Graham Evangelistic Association, or BGEA) was gaining momentum at every turn. New people had joined the team: Tedd Smith, Paul Mickelson, and T. W. Wilson (Loren Whitney and Don Hustad were still to come); while early standbys George Wilson and Willis Haymaker were devoting more and more time to this ministry.

After the Los Angeles summit we jumped to mountaintop experiences in Boston, Portland, Atlanta, and Columbia, South Carolina. Billy Graham continued to draw more and more national attention.

Henry Luce, founder of *Time* and *Life* magazines, like William Randolph Hearst, gave his stamp of approval after attending a meeting during the Columbia, South Carolina, Crusade. A team of reporters and photographers was called in the very next day to prepare a feature article for *Life*. Billy also was invited to the White House for a visit with President Truman.

On every hand there were signs of a burgeoning ministry. Opportunities came in bunches. Strong demands were made on Billy and, usually, the worthiness of the appeals caused him to acquiesce. One notable exception was the time Walter Bennett and Fred Dienert told Billy of a Sunday afternoon opening on ABC. It was a marvelous opportunity to spread the message coast to coast, they reasoned. To reserve the time for a thirteen-week contract, they told Billy that

$92,000 would be needed for air time. They urged him to give them a green light before the offer was withdrawn by the network.

Billy responded much as his Village Church board of deacons did a few years before, when he asked them for $100 a week for a radio program. Kindly but firmly, he gave Fred and Walter a negative answer. They didn't give up, however. Following him back to Montreat they appealed again, but Billy told them that a weekly program could be a full-time job; the Crusades took priority — "No, absolutely no!"

Imagine his feelings when the team of Bennett and Dienert showed up at the Portland Crusade for one last presentation: If he could raise enough to guarantee three programs — an advance of $25,000 — they could snag the time slot. After that, gifts from listeners would sustain the program, they maintained.

Billy was in a quandary. It was indeed a great opportunity, but it was also an enormous undertaking. From Howard Butt in Texas came a phone call. He had heard about the possibility of a radio program and wanted Billy to know that he and his friend Bill Mead had $1,000 each they wanted to contribute. Billy thanked them, but said that nothing definite had been decided.

Fred and Walter, who at one time spent almost a week cooling their heels, suggested that Billy tell the Portland audience about the radio opportunity.

"Boys, I think we'd better pray," Billy said.

The three of them knelt and prayed. The guidance Billy received was to "put out the fleece again."

The fleece was $25,000 by midnight. "Anything less than that," said Billy, "and the matter is closed."

At the service he told the audience of the radio offer, and of the need for $25,000 if he were to accept. He said he would be at the office behind the platform after the service, if anyone felt led to share in this proposed ministry.

At the end of the meeting, people queued up to give their support, and one by one they passed by, dropping in money and pledges — $1, $5, $10 — all the way up to a $2,500 pledge. The response was surprising and heartwarming. When the contributions and pledges were counted, they totaled $23,500 — including the $2,000 pledge from our Texas friends.

"You're on the air," somebody shouted.

Billy shook his head. The fleece had been for $25,000; $1,500 more was still needed and it was nearing midnight.

We returned to the Multnomah Hotel with mixed emotions. Billy went straight to his room, while Grady stopped at the desk. The clerk handed him three envelopes that had been left there a short time before. One envelope contained a check for $1,000; each of the others a check for $250. The three additional offerings brought the total to $25,000, right on the button. The program was assured!

Hour of Decision went on the air December 5, 1950, from Atlanta, where we were conducting a Crusade. Cliff emceed and led the singing. Jerry Beavan read Crusade news reports, Grady read the Scripture. I sang ("I'd Rather Have Jesus") and Billy gave the message.

The first program was aired over 150 stations. In five weeks it had the largest audience of any religious program in history. At the end of five years it was carried over 850 stations. George Wilson, who had hired one secretary initially to handle the mail in Minneapolis, reported an avalanche of envelopes — over 178,000 letters the first year, more than double the next.

Even more exciting than the number of letters was their content. From the mail, we learned that we were reaching a much different audience from the one that came to Crusades. The advent of tape recording enabled Cliff to build up a library of choir numbers, Grady's Scripture readings, and my solos. These he adroitly wove together with Billy's sermons. The messages are recorded each week wherever Billy may be — Manila or Montreat — to keep them as timely as today's newspaper.

The decisions that have been made for Christ as a result of the *Hour of Decision* are inestimable. And once on the air, no one on the team ever suggested that the time, money, and effort was not worth the cost.

In my twenty-one years of singing on the program I have received many letters that have moved me deeply, but none more than one I received recently. The letter was from a woman who had given up on life. Alone, in poor health, without purpose — she had decided to end it all. She lined her kitchen windows and doors with towels, turned on the gas, and sat down at the table. While she was waiting for death, she turned on the radio and the *Hour of Decision* was on.

"You were singing, 'I know not what the future holds, but I know Who holds the future.' I longed to know that Person too," she wrote. "I turned off the gas, threw open the windows, and shoved my head outside to breathe in the fresh air. I was pretty far gone, I guess. When I felt better, I sat down again at the table in time to hear Mr. Graham speaking about some of life's deep trials. Then he invited me to accept the Lord Jesus as my personal Saviour. I'm so happy to say that today I, too, know the One who holds the future."

He's got the tiny little baby in
His hands. . . .

— *He's Got the Whole World In His Hands,* Craig Starret*

20

Off to England

When 1952 rolled around, my regular duties were to sing on three weekly radio programs, two of them coast-to-coast. *Hour of Decision* and *Club Time* were heard nationwide, while *Songs in the Night* continued to be broadcast in the Chicago area over WCFL.

As the pace of Crusade work intensified and invitations to sing around the country increased, I found it more and more difficult to keep up. Just answering the mail that came in from *Club Time* listeners would have kept me busy. My time at home was limited, too, as Ronnie, who was nearing school age, reminded me one day.

"Daddy, why can't you come home every evening like Jimmy's father?" he asked.

I tried to explain that we had different kinds of jobs, but it didn't seem to satisfy him.

"Do you think I should tell Mr. Graham that I won't go with him any more?" I appealed, finally.

"Well. . . ." He wasn't sure. He ran off to play and dropped the matter — I thought. At bedtime, however, as I tucked him in he picked up the thread of the conversation again.

"Daddy, about your work — I think singing songs about Jesus for Mr. Graham is too important to quit."Then, he said his prayers and kissed me goodnight.

My prayer was a silent one, "God, show me how to use my time — at work and at home — most wisely." I knew that I would soon face another decision and I asked Him again to direct my path. He did.

Before I reached the next fork in the road, the way had been cleared and the signs posted.

Club Time came to an end in the spring of 1952, after more than eight years on the air.

The program, even at the height of its popularity, had had a limited audience, but Herbert J. Taylor had argued that the listeners were loyal and had influenced his board to keep it on the air. Now, however, a factory retooling which would take their product off the market for six months made giving up the show mandatory. With genuine concern for the program personnel, Mr. Taylor thanked everyone personally for *Club Time*'s success. All of us were deeply moved by his graciousness.

Though I was sorry to see the program end, its passing gave me the nudge needed to place myself fully at the disposal of the BGEA. A short time later I concluded eight years of *Songs in the Night,* also, and turned the mike over to Glen Jorian whose warm tenor voice has been heard on the program ever since.

The Crusade moved on — to Washington, D. C., to Memphis, to Dallas, to Detroit. Crowds grew, and so did the number of commitments to Christ. Billy's first book, *Peace with God,* rocketed to the best seller lists. He began his nationally syndicated newspaper column, "My Answer." He made a movie and a series of films for television, in which Cliff, Tedd, and I also appeared. During the peak of the Korean conflict, he visited servicemen there and also went on to Japan.

Our first Crusade abroad came in 1954. We went to London for the exhilarating Harringay meetings. (I had been, with Billy and Cliff, to England and Scotland in 1949 on a Youth for Christ trip and was anxious to return.)

Besides the blessing we received from those meetings and the warm response the people gave us, two memories stand out from that Crusade. The first was a speech we heard Sir Winston Churchill deliver in Glasgow's Ibrox Stadium. Churchill, who was making his bid for reelection, spoke before a crowd of 25,000. (We would never have gotten into the stadium had it not been for a doctor friend of Billy's.) We listened, enthralled, as this man of history talked for over seventy minutes.

"All my goals have been achieved," he told his countrymen. "I have no reason to go back to Parliament, but I must." Then he spoke passionately and movingly of what England meant to him, and why he felt he must serve her to his death. When he had finished, we joined in the thunderous applause. Clapping hard, I looked over at

Billy, through my own tears, only to discover trickles running down *his* cheeks.

"He's got my vote," Billy shouted, getting out his handkerchief.

"Mine, too," I answered. "But I can't understand *you*. I'm a Canadian by birth; I have a right to wave the flag, but how can a tarheel from North Carolina get so worked up over British politics?"

The other poignant memory of that trip was visiting Edinburgh's Carrubbers Close Mission, which was built from profits of songbooks sold by the team of Dwight L. Moody and Ira D. Sankey. In one building of the mission I sat down and played on the very reed organ (the Scots called it a "kist o'whustles") Sankey had used to introduce his composition "The Ninety and Nine." (This organ was later given to the BGEA and is now housed in Minneapolis.)

It was at the mission that I learned how this classic hymn came to be written.

Moody and Sankey were traveling by train to Edinburgh for two days of meetings. While Moody scribbled answers to letters which had been forwarded from Chicago, Sankey read a newspaper. In the paper he came upon a poem, "The Lost Sheep."

"If this poem had a tune, it might make a fine hymn," he told the evangelist.

"Read it to me, Sankey."

Sankey gave a spirited reading of the poem, but Moody had become so engrossed in his mail he didn't hear a word of it. With a frown, Sankey tore the verse from the paper and put it in his notebook.

The next afternoon the title of Moody's message was "The Good Shepherd." After he had spoken, Moody turned to his vocalist and asked hurriedly, "Have you got something appropriate to finish the service with?"

Sankey thought. He had sung a a metrical version of the 23rd Psalm already so he did not want to repeat that.

Suddenly, he remembered the poem he had found in the paper. "Sing that hymn," a voice seemed to say. "But it is no hymn — it has no music," Sankey answered himself.

Moody turned to Sankey again, "Well?"

Reaching into the book of music, Sankey found the poem and placed it on the music rack of the little organ. Striking a chord in the key of A flat, he began to sing the hymn that was soon to find its way into the hearts of people the world over:

> There were ninety and nine that safely lay
>   In the shelter of the fold,
> But one was out on the hills away,
>   Far off from the gates of gold —
> Away on the mountains wild and bare,
>   Away from the tender Shepherd's care,
> Away from the tender Shepherd's care.

The audience was touched and seemed to move en masse to the edge of their chairs. Sankey moved to the edge of his chair, too. But his reason was suspense. He had sung the first verse, but he wasn't sure he could remember the music well enough to do the second. But he began — haltingly at first, then more confidently. He made it through all five verses, and a new hymn was born.

Though England itself was not the inspiration for a hymn I wrote, a trip to England was to figure in it. Aboard the S.S. United States on our way to London, a man who had never been to a Crusade asked me one afternoon, "What goes on at your meetings?"

I tried to describe a typical service — Billy's preaching, Cliff's songleading, Tedd's playing — but when I attempted to tell him about the invitation at the end of the service, my tongue froze, I had no words. "Oh, if you could just see it . . . the — the wonder of it all."

In our cabin that night, I told Erma about the experience, including my difficulty in painting a word picture of the invitation. After we went to bed, my conversation with this man kept coming back to mind. Finally, about 2 A.M., I got up and began writing on the back of a ship's laundry list. What I wrote was the words and music to a hymn that you may have heard, "The Wonder of It All."

The famous Harringay Crusade, held in North London's Harringay arena, has been well documented in other books. All I can add is a personal note or two. During the three months of meetings, an unprecedented number for us — more than 38,000 — came forward and gave their lives to Christ.

One story that moved me deeply was of a man who came to a service under duress, as a favor to a friend. He was not in sympathy with our evangelistic approach and he made it known to the people around him. At every opportunity he heckled those on the platform.

He made fun of Grady when he read the Scriptures, ridiculed Cliff when he led the choir and the audience in song.

"Somebody's making a haul," he said sarcastically, when the collection was taken.

When I stood to sing, I understand he made a wisecrack, too. But midway through my number, "He's Got the Whole World in His Hands," I'm told, the man grew serious and bowed his head. It was at the point in the song where I cradle my arms and talk the words in a whisper, "He's got the tiny little baby in His hands. . . ."

After my song, Billy spoke and the scoffer listened to every word without a sound. When the invitation was given, he walked forward to give his life to God. It was in the inquiry room that counselors learned his story. He had a seriously ill child at home, and the words of that tender song had touched his heart.

The meetings culminated at Wembley Stadium, where 120,000 people flooded into the 67,000-seat arena — the overflow standing on the infield.

Over two thousand persons responded to the invitation that final night and after the service the press crowded around Billy for a statement evaluating the Crusade.

"It is too early to make an assessment," he answered. "We leave the results in His hands."

The team managed to get through the crowd and into the bus to go back to our hotel. But before we pulled out of the parking area, Billy stood and asked us to join him in prayer, thanking God for the work He had done.

When he finished, we began "Praise God from Whom All Blessings Flow." Like a football team fresh from a big victory, we were full of the unexcelled joy that comes from a triumph shared with Christ.

Then sings my soul, my Saviour God, to Thee:
   How great Thou art, How great Thou art!
Then sings my soul, my Saviour God, to Thee:
   How great Thou art, How great Thou art!
— *How Great Thou Art*

21

Then Sings My Soul

Returning from England and Scotland, I brought back a copy of a hymn which had been given me by my friend George Gray, of the well-known religious book publishing house, Pickering and Inglis, Limited. I was out walking on London's Oxford Street one day when I bumped into Mr. Gray. As we chatted he reached into his briefcase and pulled out a leaflet on which were printed the words and music to a "new" hymn.

"Here is something you might like to sing at Harringay," Mr. Gray suggested.

I glanced over the lyrics and music and could see that the hymn had majesty and power to it.

"This looks good," I told him. "Are we free to use it?"

"Certainly," he said.

He gave Cliff a copy also, but our schedule was too hectic to consider a new arrangement and rehearsal in London. So the song was packed away among my things, and it was not until two or three months after our return to the States that I sang it for the first time.

One day at home I was sorting through some notes and came across the leaflet Mr. Gray had given me.

Sitting down at the piano, I played and sang it through:

O Lord my God, when I in awesome wonder
   Consider all the worlds Thy hands have made,
I see the stars, I hear the rolling thunder,
   Thy power throughout the Universe displayed;

When Christ shall come with shout of acclamation
   And take me home, what joy shall fill my heart!
Then I shall bow in humble adoration,
   And there proclaim, my God, how great Thou art!

It was beautiful!

I couldn't wait to do it in a Crusade and mentioned "How Great Thou Art" to Cliff the next time we were together. His face brightened because he had played it over himself and he shared my enthusiasm. Tedd Smith and Paul Mickelson were given copies and they worked out an arrangement which we sang for the first time at Maple Leaf Garden in 1955, during the Toronto Crusade.

One night I arrived at the arena early, and off in the distance I could hear the choir rehearsing "How Great Thou Art." When I reached the platform, Cliff turned to me and called out, "We're ready, Bev."

"So am I," I answered and together we rehearsed it.

The response was unbelievable. The S. K. Hine translation of the hymn had first been brought to the United States by Dr. Edwin Orr in 1951, and was much appreciated by his audiences. But after the Toronto Crusade and its *Hour of Decision* exposure, its popularity spread across the country with such frenzy that it soon became one of the most popular hymns in America. It wasn't long, of course, until it was being sung all over the world.

Requests to hear it flooded in. We did it as often as we thought prudent on the *Hour of Decision* and, every time, George Wilson's mailbag in Minneapolis would be filled with letters from new hearers.

"Sing it again," they would write.

"Where can I buy the music?"

"Has Bev Shea recorded it?"

(The answer to that last question is "Yes, three times, for RCA.")

They kept writing, wiring, phoning, "We are coming to the Crusade Tuesday night and bringing a whole busload. Have Bev Shea and the choir sing 'How Great Thou Art'." Never has such a number received such overwhelming approval at the Crusades.

All this excitement over the hymn made me wonder about its history. I discovered that Stuart K. Hine had all the facts at hand.

The first surprise was that this "new hymn" by Mr. Hine was about seventy years old. Written in Sweden in 1885 or 1886 by the Reverend Carl Boberg, a noted preacher and religious editor, it was originally titled *"O Store Gud"* ("O Great God").

The first translation into English, published in 1925, was entitled "O Mighty God." "How Great Thou Art" had had an even more circuitous route.

It had been translated from Swedish to German in 1907 by Manfred von Glehn of Estonia. In 1912, the Reverend Ivan S. Prokhanoff, who has been called "the Martin Luther of Russia," translated it into Russian — probably from the German version. In 1922, a book of Prokhanoff's hymns was published in Russian by the American Bible Society in New York City. It was included in another, larger hymnal published in America five years later.

It was the second book of hymns that fell into the hands of an English missionary couple, Mr. and Mrs. Stuart K. Hine. They used "How Great Thou Art" with fine results in their missionary work in the Ukraine.

After several years of use in Russia, Mr. Hine translated the first three verses of it into English. When World War II began, he returned to Britain and added the fourth stanza in 1948. The song, now complete, was printed in a Russian gospel magazine published by Mr. Hine in 1949. This magazine was read by missionaries all over the world and numerous requests came for copies. Mr. Hine had some leaflets printed and it was one of those leaflets that Mr. Gray gave me in London in 1954. A long story, but an interesting one to those of us who have been so greatly blessed by the hymn's powerful message. Mr. Hine, of course, is the one who deserves our thanks, for through his work the entire world has been given an all-time religious classic. (And I would be remiss if I didn't mention the significant role of Tim Spencer, President of Manna Music, Inc., publishers of the hymn in North America.)

At the great 1957 Crusade in New York's Madison Square Garden, I sang "How Great Thou Art" with the choir a total of ninety-nine times. It became the unofficial theme song of that Crusade, and once again we received letter after letter from people blessed by the song's moving message.

Singing any number that often can sometimes cause us to lose the full impact of the words. I remember one night toward the end of the Madison Square Garden meeting when my weariness got the best of me. I caught myself mouthing the words rather than singing them from the heart.

In my room that night, I had a talk with the Lord, "Father, please forgive me for my apathy in singing that great hymn this evening," I prayed. "I promise it won't happen again."

And it hasn't.

It took a miracle to put the stars in place,
It took a miracle to hang the world in space. . . .
— *It Took a Miracle,* John Peterson*

22

In the Garden

I don't want to pass over the Madison Square Garden Crusade in
1957 with the lightweight footnote that we sang "How Great Thou
Art" ninety-nine times. That is one of the least significant statistics of
all the figures compiled on the mammoth New York meetings.

One is often impressed with statistics, but sometimes I think that
Screwtape is overjoyed when Christians get hung up on them. Nonetheless, for the record, here are a few of the impressive marks that
were reached that summer:

Scheduled for six weeks, the Crusade ran for sixteen.
Attendance at the rate of about 19,000 a night ran approximately two
million all told.
More than 60,000 came forward when the invitation was given.
Better than 65,000 were known to have made commitments after they
watched one of the fourteen Saturday-night television programs.

But the thrill of it all cannot be told in numbers. The real story of
the Crusade can be told only by the individuals who came and
listened and acted. Many moving experiences were brought to the attention of the team that summer, but none pulled my heartstrings
more than a story Charlie Riggs told. (Charlie, with Dan Piatt and
Lorne Sanny, did a great job training counselors at the New York
Crusade.)

In the inquiry room one night, a simply dressed woman from a
tenement accepted the Lord into her life. Tears of release are not un-

common at such a time, but her crying was punctuated by sobs and intermittent petitions of "God, protect me."

When a counselor asked her if there was something more she wished to talk about, the woman told of her son's hatred for the church.

"He drinks a lot," she said, "and I'm afraid he may beat me when he finds out I've become a Christian."

Before the counselor could speak, a voice nearby called out, "It's okay, Mom. I'm here too."

Living in New York that summer was a wonderful homecoming for Erma and me. It had been nineteen years since we had left Manhattan for Chicago — under a little different circumstances. So many old acquaintances came to the meetings and stayed afterward to talk. Such friends as Will and Laura Ebner, Ma and Pa Hopper, who took Erma and me into their home for a few months when our finances had been in need of a tourniquet; Mr. and Mrs. J. Thurston Noé, Price Boone, and many of the old friends from the Jersey City church.

One morning I took a cab to see the old gang at the new MONY offices uptown on Broadway and 57th Street. There were many familiar faces still around the medical department, including Dr. Willis, Dr. Moore, and Dr. Russell. My old boss, Harold Voege, had retired and Charles Van Riper was now chief clerk. Charley said he had heard from Mr. Voege recently; he had wanted to come to New York to attend the meetings, but couldn't because of his wife's illness.

"He told me once," Charley recalled, "that 'to hear Bev use his voice for the Lord is the answer to my prayers'." It sounded like Harold.

The President of MONY, Roger Hull, served as chairman of the Crusade executive committee and he did a tremendous organizational job. The New York meetings were the most elaborately organized I had ever seen and, starting with advance work right through to the last meeting, almost everything clicked with the precision of a crack drill team.

We certainly had a group of dedicated people serving the Lord that summer. All told, there were twenty-two members on the official team, but fourteen others were commissioned from our "taxi squad." As you know, in professional football that's the name for the reserves who are called in when reinforcements are needed, and our team was bolstered considerably by these strong friends.

One fellow who was activated especially for the New York meetings was Lane Adams. Lane was still in a Presbyterian seminary then, but he was already a mature Christian leader. Regular team-member-

to-be Lane, a former nightclub entertainer, was given an unusual assignment: show business. Billy knew that many show people in New York had strong religious convictions, and he sought their support of our meetings.

Certainly an impressive galaxy of personalities showed up during the course of those meetings. They came from about every field imaginable — the theater, movies, radio, television, writing, politics, sports. Among the names I remember were Vice-President Richard Nixon, Ed Sullivan, Sonja Henie, Gene Tierney, Greer Garson, Dale Evans, Perle Mesta, Pearl Bailey, Jack Dempsey, Alvin Dark, Carl Erskine, Walter Winchell, Dorothy Kilgallen, Ethel Waters. . . .

Miss Waters' contribution to the Crusade was a substantial one. In addition to singing in the 2,000-voice choir every night save one, she was called upon to do "His Eye Is On the Sparrow" many, many times. What a stirring testimony she gave with that old song as she sang, "I know he watches WE."

When Miss Waters sang, I always thought of a sage observation Ira Sankey made, "Many a man will come to church and the sermon will pass into and out of his mind and it will be forgotten; but the hymn will linger and work for good." Ethel Waters sings from the bottom of her heart, and immeasurable power flows from her voice. It works for God — and for good in all who hear.

Lane Adams not only succeeded in finding people in show business to lend their support, he brought them together and laid the groundwork for the New York Christian Arts Fellowship. Jerome Hines, Metropolitan Opera basso, served as first president of the group. Jerome, chairman of our music committee and a long-time friend of mine, was of outstanding help during the Crusade. It was a great blessing to hear him give his witness in song.

I remember one night Jerome invited me backstage at the old Met. He sat in his dressing room before a production of *Don Giovanni* (in which he had the title role) and talked right up until curtain time. I made several moves toward the door, thinking he would want a period of quiet before going on the stage, but each time he motioned for me to stay.

"Relax, Bev, there's still plenty of time for you to get to your seat."

Finally, the stage manager called, "Five minutes, Mr. Hines," and we went outside — Jerome in heavy makeup and elaborate costume. Just as we stepped out of his dressing room door, Impresario Rudolf Bing came down the passageway.

"Mr. Bing," Jerome said, "I'd like you to meet my good friend, George Beverly Shea, who sings for Billy Graham."

As Mr. Bing shook my hand he made an aside to Jerome, "He may make it yet." An impish twinkle sparkled in his eyes as he bade us good-bye.

Jerome burst out laughing and then said with great diplomacy, "To Mr. Bing there is only one Big League."

So many memories flood my mind as I think back to those days. . . . The time the team spent at Wainwright House in Rye, New York — just off Long Island Sound — before the New York Crusade. I was there as we laid our final strategy for invading the Big Town with the message of Christ. All our doubts and fears came to a head and our confidence was quavery until two team members from England — Ralph Mitchell and Joe Blinco — put our thinking straight.

"If we had to go into New York alone, we would have cause to be apprehensive," Ralph told us in a moving devotional one day. "But we have a Leader whose presence will strengthen us if we seek Him out prayerfully."

Still we vacillated between supreme confidence and knee-knocking doubt right up until the meetings began. About five o'clock in the afternoon, just a few hours before the opening service, the phone rang. It was Billy. He had been struck by feelings of doubt and he wanted some prayer partners.

"Please come down to my room, Bev," said Billy. "I'm going to call Cliff, Grady, and some others."

A few minutes later half a dozen team members knelt together and asked God for reassurance. He gave it later that night — in the form of 19,000 people who crammed into Madison Square Garden to hear the Gospel. That night, and throughout the rest of the Crusade, we proclaimed it as simply and directly as we knew how. Any preconceptions our people had had about "ultrasophisticated" New Yorkers were wiped away in the weeks of warm fellowship that followed.

One of our most moving experiences took place at Yankee Stadium on July 21. That meeting was attended by over 100,000 people and 20,000 more were turned away. Vice-President Richard Nixon brought personal greetings from President Eisenhower, whom Billy had visited just before the opening of the New York meetings.

Looking over the huge throng that day, I can remember the strains of "How Great Thou Art" reverberating through that cavernous arena. When the choir joined me on the chorus, it sounded as if all the angels in heaven were lending their voices.

On the final climactic night in Times Square on Labor Day weekend, estimates of the crowd ran from 160,000 to 200,000. All *I* know is that there were more people in one spot than I have ever seen in my life.

After Billy's Spirit-charged message, the choir sang "Just As I Am." Once upon a time, Billy used to ask the congregation to join in on the invitational hymn. But after I told him about my experience as a boy — how I sang away my conviction in lieu of going to the altar — the choir sang the invitation alone. That is the way it was in Times Square.

In the streets of the city there was no room to move forward, so Billy asked those who wanted to receive Christ into their lives to raise their hands. From the acres of tightly packed bodies, thousands of hands reached up — hands that represented every ethnic background in the world. All those who accepted Christ that night were asked to send postcards, including their names and addresses, so that follow-up workers could refer them to local churches.

As the service ended, the electric news ribbon that circled Times Tower flashed the headlines: *Billy Graham Crusade Ends in Times Square Rally.* The meetings had come to an end, but I knew that the spirit of them had not — and would not.

The miracle of rebirth in Christ would spread in the years ahead just as the people who had come and received Him were now fanning out across that sprawling metropolis. I watched them go — downtown toward the Lower East Side, Wall Street, Greenwich Village, Brooklyn, Staten Island, New Jersey; uptown through the Great White Way toward Harlem, the Bronx, Queens, Westchester, and beyond.

As I scanned that emblazoned panorama, my eyes were drawn from the streets to a huge sign atop one of the buildings. It was advertising the insurance company for which I once had worked. Suddenly, I was aware — more aware than ever before — of the miracle God had wrought in my life. He had been able to use a simple psalm singer such as I — that was a miracle, nothing less. I could not understand it, then or now. All I could do was praise Him for His presence in my life, as I had done that night in song:

> It took a miracle to put the stars in place,
> It took a miracle to hang the world in space.
> But when He saved my soul,
> Cleansed and made it whole,
> It took a miracle of love and grace.

What a friend we have in Jesus,
All our sins and griefs to bear,
What a privilege to carry
Everything to God in prayer.
— Joseph Scriven

23

A Full Mailbox

After our next trip to England, Billy received a letter from a very distraught lady critical of him for bringing a soloist to her country's shores who had the audacity to sing:

> **It took *America* to put the stars in place,**
> **It took *America* to hang the world in space!**

I have no idea what Billy's answer was, but my response was to be more careful with enunciation of that phrase. Wars have been started over less!

But write people do. After the New York Crusade, mail increased for every team member. George Wilson reported that over 1,500,000 letters came into BGEA headquarters in Minneapolis as a result of the New York TV programs alone. This response made us decide to use TV as a regular part of Crusade ministry thereafter.

Whatever the source — Crusades, *Hour of Decision,* television, recordings, or the *Evening of Sacred Music* concerts which I do on occasion, with Tedd Smith or Don Hustad — the mail flows in, and it covers most all subjects. One woman wrote not long ago, "Please, Mr. Shea, don't wear those horrible looking dark-rimmed glasses. They don't help a bit."

If she only knew how much they do help! Apparently, she was not a student of hymns, or she would have noticed how small the type is that sheet music publishers are using these days. It must be half the size it was twenty years ago!

Many people send in compositions, asking to have them recorded. One appreciates the spirit in which most of them are sent, but I must return all music and all poetry with the suggestion that the author submit his work to a reputable publisher first, who, if the composition has merit, will arrange to copyright, publish, and distribute it. Most singers will not consider using a song until these steps have been completed.

I must confess that I am greatly tempted to intervene at times — some mighty fine lyrics come to our attention. The thoughts of many of the poems are excellent, but the verse often needs refinement. I loved the depth of feeling expressed in one recent submission, yet somehow could not imagine myself singing a hymn entitled, "His Grip Don't Slip." I guess I'm just an old square.

One of the most difficult letters to answer is one asking for career advice. I am a poor one to give guidance counseling. First of all, I stopped a little short of the prescribed formal schooling I consider a requisite for a career in music; second, my own route has been rather unorthodox.

Generally, I try to make the following points when answering an aspiring vocalist, organist, pianist, choir director, or composer:

1. And this *is* number one! Pray that God will direct your path. "Does God want this for me?" is the most important question you can ask yourself.

2. Serve where you are with all your heart. You can serve God anywhere. Do the job before you well and other opportunities may blossom because of it. Milton gave us all good advice, "They also serve who only stand and wait." I don't mean that you should expect a windfall without effort. I do mean what someone said long ago, that God supplies birds with their food, but He does not put it in their nests.

3. "Study to show thyself approved unto God . . ." is a good rule; another one follows in the same verse: ". . . a workman that needeth not to be ashamed. . . ." (II Timothy 2:15). Polish and improve whatever God has given you until it becomes more worthy of Him.

4. Dream big. God has a way of honoring people who dream of serving Him in a task bigger than they can handle alone. Have faith that God's plan is at work, this minute, in your life.

The right attitude is vitally important in working for the Lord. My idea of a perfect approach to serving God can best be illustrated by an experience I had not long ago.

Just before I went to the platform at a Crusade, a teen-age girl asked me, "How do I get into this *business*? My friends say I wow 'em when I sing a hymn."

I was thrown by her brashness but tried not to show it. "Let me ask you a question," I said. "Do you want to sing for the Lord or for yourself? First, you must decide which it is to be. You pray about it."

After the service, when I was leaving the platform, a young man of twenty or twenty-one approached me. "Tell me, Mr. Shea, that song you sing just before Mr. Graham preaches, how do you choose it — through prayer?"

I told him that I always looked to the Lord for guidance in choosing that one. He smiled. "I thought so. I love to sing, too, Mr. Shea, and some day I hope I'll be doing what you are. Pray that God will lead me."

Most of my letters are invitations to sing at various affairs around the country. The real dilemma is to choose which I can accept. Because I can seldom say "No," the BGEA has taken on the task for me. All my appointments are made under the auspices of the BGEA and all monies received go back to that organization. All team members work on a salary basis.

I love to sing and chat with the people who attend our *Evening of Sacred Music* concerts, which we have been doing at the rate of about twelve a year. (These are, of course, in addition to our Crusade work.) Some of the classics such as "How Lovely Are Thy Dwellings," "Green Pastures," "Remember Now Thy Creator," and "The Earth is the Lord's" are numbers I seldom do in a Crusade. Tedd, Don, and I have received some wonderful welcomes on our concert trips both here and abroad, and we've had some great times together, too.

I won't forget an experience we had in Nova Scotia recently. While I was singing to an audience of several hundred, my accompaniment stopped — I was suddenly performing a cappella! Continuing as if nothing had happened, I was still puzzled. Where was Tedd? Had he gone out for a cup of coffee? I sneaked a glance at the piano. Like Mother Hubbard's cupboard, the piano bench was bare. I finished up as best I could. Then I turned toward the piano, determined to solve the mystery of my missing partner.

I saw a rather macabre sight — one lone hand hooked awkwardly over the keys. Tedd was sitting under the keyboard, struggling valiantly with the foot pedals. The audience saw it all and roared with laughter. Tedd did not see the humor in the situation.

"See if there is a piano repairman in the house," he called to me in a stage whisper.

Much to my surprise, one stepped out of the crowd and within a few minutes solved the difficulty. Tedd, by now in better spirits,

dusted off his trousers, regained his composure, and continued to play — in the normal position!

One letter that didn't take me long to answer was one from Dr. Richard Halverson of International Christian Leadership. It was an invitation to sing at the annual President's Prayer Breakfast. What a privilege it has been to sing at these breakfasts — once before President Eisenhower and once before President Johnson.

The first time was impromptu. I was in the audience having breakfast with Russell Hitt when Abraham Vereide came over to our table and asked if I would lead the group in "What A Friend We Have in Jesus."

As mentioned before, I never eat heavily before singing, but here I had little choice. Though I had just finished a huge breakfast, I stood and led some nine hundred people in singing that old hymn. President Eisenhower was standing right at my elbow and he joined in, but I was too nervous to even glance in his direction.

The next day I saw the scene captured on videotape on the *Today* show — old psalm singer Shea right next to the President! One thing for sure: the President knew the lyrics well. Billy, who spoke that day, told me some time later that the President had requested the hymn, which was his favorite.

"By the way," Billy asked, "why did you refuse to shake hands with the President? You left him with his hand waving in the breeze."

"Refuse?" I answered in surprise. "I didn't see him offer his hand. I guess I was too nervous to notice."

A few months later there came a chance to redeem myself. I was invited back to Washington to sing at the annual convention of the National Christian Endeavor. Again the President was to be on hand. Ill-health kept Billy Graham from honoring the speaking engagement, so Cliff spoke for him. And what a curve they threw Cliff!

Because he had other commitments, the President was not able to be present at the beginning of the program but was expected later. Cliff began his remarks but was interrupted in midstream by a secret service man who marched across the platform with a wooden plaque bearing the Presidential seal. Valiantly, Cliff continued his speech while the aide tacked the insignia to the front of the lectern. Poor Cliff — there he was, speaking in front of a sign that read, "The President of the United States!" A wag commented, "In America it can happen to any boy — any time."

Cliff brought his speech to a hasty close and the President, who we all knew was waiting in the wings, was ushered to the rostrum. We all figured he would make a short courtesy talk and leave. After he

finished, however, he whispered to Dr. Dan Poling that he'd like to stay for a while.

So Dr. Poling motioned for me to go ahead with my song. Again the President was close by. *This* time I vowed I'd not miss his handshake — if he offered it.

After I'd finished "I'd Rather Have Jesus," I passed the President, but he had joined the audience in applauding so I couldn't shake his hand. I gave him a squeeze on the shoulder instead, as I walked back to my seat.

(Later, Grady Wilson said, with a grin, "Don't you know nothin', man? I expected to see some secret service man plug you right between the eyes. You can't put your hands on the President like that!")

When Mr. Eisenhower rose to leave, we all stood and clapped. He shook hands with all of those nearby, turned to go — and then spotted me across the way. To my great surprise and pleasure, he crossed the dais and shook my hand!

"Thank you so much for that hymn, Mr. Shea," he said.

"You're very gracious, Mr. President," I answered. It was quite a thrill!

In later years, postmarks have come from more and more distant lands as the Billy Graham Crusade has moved in wider and wider circles. There are a number of places where I have not sung in person but, in most of those, Armed Forces Radio, the *Hour of Decision,* TV films, or RCA recordings have made the trip for me.

Not long ago I marked on a map the countries in which I have been privileged to sing the Gospel — such farflung lands as Scotland, England, France, Finland, Sweden, Germany, Australia, New Zealand, Hawaii, Taiwan, Vietnam, Costa Rica, Ecuador, and Canada.

Though I have received many warm and moving letters from around the globe, I have a few favorites. Among them is a letter from Dave Morken, a former American missionary to China who later joined with Bob Pierce and World Vision. (The letter came some time after the fall of Shanghai, but its significance is heightened by its later perspective on the incident.)

"There were many Westerners who had chosen to stay," Dave wrote me, "even though they knew what was coming. As time grew short, many of them turned their radios to the English-speaking station and listened to my program, the final fifteen minutes of free speech to be broadcast before the Red takeover. I read a passage of Scripture, gave a short farewell message and then for the benediction, I played your recording of 'If We Could See Beyond Today.'

"Those were the final words to go out across the air:

If we could see beyond today as God can see,
If all the clouds should roll away, the shadows flee;
O'er present griefs, we would not fret,
Each sorrow we would soon forget,
For many joys are waiting yet
For you and me.

— (Words and Music Copyright 1943, Norman Clayton Publishing Company, Owner. Used by permission.)

"In the many black days that followed, Bev, the words of that song did more than anything else to sustain people's hope and courage."

Another "keepsake" letter came from Vietnam after Billy, Cliff, Dan Piatt, Tedd, and I visited servicemen there over Christmas, 1966. It was a rather awkwardly written note — a simple thank you from a soldier whose Christmas had somehow been made less bleak by our service — but the chord of courage and faith it struck moved me deeply. It also called to mind that unforgettable Christmas Eve.

I can still see the scene in the Central Highlands. After fifty-seven days in the thick of things, the boys came off the lines for the Christmas truce. Many of them, of course, had to stand guard that Christmas Eve night and were not able to attend our service at An Khe. We visited some of them.

A lieutenant drove me around the area in his jeep. We stopped at a spot where the tents were pitched in a giant circle around a brightly decorated Christmas tree. The gaily wrapped presents beneath it seemed incongruous in that drab setting. Though the weather was threatening, many of the soldiers stood outside of their tents, talking. The lieutenant introduced me and I had a pleasant chat with many of the boys. I recorded some names and phone numbers of parents, wives, girl friends, and pals to call when I got back to the States. Then, across the way, where a number of soldiers were lined up waiting for a haircut, someone yelled, "Hey, Mr. Shea, sing something for us." Others chimed in.

"What would you like to hear?" I called out. I could have guessed. Nearly in unison they answered, "How Great Thou Art."

They gave the hymn a good hand afterwards. Then I piled back into the jeep and waved good-bye.

By the time we got back to our quarters at An Khe, the rain was drenching the countryside and we were all concerned about the service scheduled for 8 o'clock. It was still coming down in buckets at 7

o'clock . . . 7:30 . . . 7:45. Suddenly, without warning, the downpour stopped minutes before eight, and the hillside designated for the meeting began to fill up with soldiers.

A Catholic chaplain had arranged for each man to be given a paper cup in which a small candle had been placed. When the service began, we looked out on thousands of faces, each one lighted by a candle.

It was a moving service. The men sang heartily and beautifully when Cliff led them in carols; they listened intently as Billy talked about the hope of Christmas. For my number I chose that old favorite, "I Heard the Bells on Christmas Day":

> **And in despair I bowed my head;**
> **"There is no peace on earth," I said,**
> **"For hate is strong, and mocks the song**
> **Of peace on earth good will to men."**
> **Then pealed the bells more loud and deep:**
> **"God is not dead, nor doth He sleep;**
> **The wrong shall fail, the right prevail**
> **With peace on earth, good will to men."**

Less than three hours later the peace that enfolded that hillside of American young men was broken. Cracking mortars announced the end of the truce. After a perfunctory nod in observance of Christ's birth, the war went on.

If I am dreaming, let me dream on.
— Gypsy Smith

24

. . . And from Here?

One morning not long ago Billy and I were out for a morning walk through the enchanting streets of Lyons, France.

"Billy, how long do you think I'm going to be able to keep up with you?" I asked.

He stopped and said apologetically, "I'm sorry, Bev, I didn't realize I was walking so fast."

"That's not what I mean. How long do you think I'm going to be able to keep going in this work?"

"Why Bev," he answered seriously, "I want you to sing for me all your life."

"I'd like that," I told him.

And I would. Singing is my life, and I hope that I can serve the Lord with my voice, in some way, for many years to come. Yet I realize that the day will dawn when it will be better for everyone if I do all my singing "down behind the barn," where I first sang as a boy. If I feel that God wants me to stop I won't resist Him for a moment. Not that I think that that time is imminent — for never in my life has God opened as many doors as He has in the past two or three years. Opportunities have come to me that I never expected; I am still awed by the responsibilities He has placed on my shoulders. Yet with the additional challenges, He has given new strength, new insight, new friends, and sustaining old friends.

It is working with Billy Graham and the members of his dedicated team that makes it all such a joy. I never cease to thank the Lord for this privilege. To Billy most of all, I shall be eternally grateful. What

a wonderful experience to know this great 24-hour-a-day Christian — and be able to call him "my friend."

Now I would not deny that I sometimes tire of all the demands. Anyone who has to travel in his job knows that moving around on airplanes, living out of suitcases, and eating meals on the run is an exhausting regimen. We all need regular respites from this grind.

A few years ago Erma and I found an idyllic setting on a placid lake in Quebec. We acquired an acre-and-a-quarter island near the area in which I grew up. On it we have put up a rustic 39-by-24-foot prefab cabin, which now serves as our vacation headquarters, and it could serve as a little more regular hideaway if we so chose.

The problem at the moment is finding time to use it. Our intentions are always good — we begin by planning to spend several weeks there every summer. Then our singing schedule expands like an accordion, and our "several" weeks narrows to two or three. Last summer we settled for two weeks; the year before, we managed four.

When I lamented this fact to a doctor friend of mine, he gave me some good advice, "I tell my patients it is good therapy to think about such a place, even if you don't get there often." On the average, I have fifty weeks of therapy and two weeks of realization!

One of the greatest joys the cabin offers us is family unity. Ron and Lainie are both in college now, so we don't get to spend as much time with them as we would like. The cabin brings us together; it's like old times. Children help us keep our perspective and our sense of humor.

I remember an incident a few summers back. Lainie and I stopped off at the drugstore for milk shakes. The place was crowded.

"A double chocolate, please, extra thick," I told the girl behind the counter.

"But Daddy," Lainie scolded, in a voice all could hear. "You just had your Metrecal!"

We have a small motor boat that serves as pleasure craft, ski tower, fishing boat, swimming and sunning raft. We also have a small sailboat which affords us a lot of fun.

Often, in the mornings, I'll take our little sailboat out on the lake and just listen to the singing of the wind and water. I never seem to get far away from music, though at the lake I'm a little lost without the instruments and sound facilities we enjoy at home.

After vacation time is over and school begins again, Erma and I return home with Laddie, our collie; Trix, a run-of-the-house cat; and my stereo equipment. We still live in the same house Billy and Ruth led us to twenty-four years ago, though we have added on to it four times. The last addition was for me — a kind of studio where I

keep an electronic organ, a piano, a large collection of symphonic and sacred records, and a stereo system that is capable of filling the room (and house) with a mighty big sound.

The location of our house is ideal — about fifteen minutes by freeway southwest of O'Hare Airport, which is my second home. For the past twenty years about half of my life seems to have been spent going to or coming from the airport. Not long ago someone asked me how many miles we log a year and it would be difficult to venture a guess. (Since then, I have done some figuring and have come up with an average of about 60,000 miles a year.)

The house at Western Springs is also a museum for scores of artifacts I have lugged home from around the world. Leather hassocks from Costa Rica, German cuckoo clocks, strange looking musical instruments from Australia, ad nauseam.

There are also two new pieces of gold-plated hardware that have been added to our collection recently. Both are awards I received in 1966. The first one is a trophy presented by RCA Victor in recognition of the great selling job they have done on my records. In 1966 my long-playing record albums went over the one-million mark, and some of my good friends at RCA surprised me with a little party in Hollywood.

The second award, which occupies a special spot in the Shea home, is a much coveted "Grammy," the recording industry's equivalent to an Oscar. The nomination had been tendered for the recording of "Southland Favorites." I made the album in Nashville with the Anita Kerr Singers, who also received a "Grammy." (They did magnificently with the background of such hymns as "Peace in the Valley," "Precious Memories," "The Last Mile of the Way," "The Eastern Gates," and "Why Should He Love Me So?")

Though nominated for the award by the National Association of Recording Arts and Sciences five times in the sacred music category, there is some powerful, stiff competition for this award and I have won it only once. If you consider the previous winners' list, which includes Tennessee Ernie Ford, Kate Smith, and Mahalia Jackson, you'll understand why!

I shall never forget the way I learned of the award. Darol Rice, another great A&R man, encouraged me to attend one of the dinners — held simultaneously in New York, Chicago, Nashville, and Hollywood.

"This may be the year, Bev," he encouraged me when I told him I was not planning to attend. "Okay, I'll pick up the award for you."

"Sure, you do that," I answered with a laugh.

The night of the banquet came and went and, as in the past, I heard nothing — just as I expected. But the next day I was out in the garage trying to fix the power mower when a taxi pulled up in the driveway. The cab driver came toward the house, and I went out to meet him, wiping black, greasy hands on my overalls.

"I have a telegram for a Mr. Shea," he said.

I took it, thanked him, walked up the front steps, and opened it. The first thing I saw was Darol's name; the second was "You won!" I ran into the house, calling to Erma. She couldn't make much of my excited jabbering until I handed her the telegram. Then *she* started jabbering. We celebrated with a cup of coffee and a stale Danish roll!

While we were still in the kitchen, Darol called from Los Angeles to give me the details. He reviewed the highlights of the previous evening from the beginning all the way through to his acceptance of the award in my behalf from Jerry Lewis.

"We're proud of you, boy," he exclaimed.

"Well, the award belongs to you too, Darol. You know, I always have hoped that someday I would become a grandfather, but I never expected to be a grammy!"

He broke up on that one and hung up. Apparently he passed the pun on to the press, because the next day I read the line in the papers.

Another honor that came my way a few years before the Grammy was an honorary degree from Houghton College. That was also a big surprise, considering that GBS was never much of a student and that he had attended Houghton for only one year. I had planned to return after I saved some money, but one thing led to another and I never quite made it.

After President Stephen Paine presented me with the honorary doctorate on the Houghton campus that June day — the same day my former boss Herbert J. Taylor received a doctorate — I told an old friend something that might be worth repeating.

"I'm reminded of Gypsy Smith's song 'If I Am Dreaming, Let Me Dream On'," I said. "So many wonderful things have happened to me — things I haven't deserved — that I often suspect I am dreaming. If my suspicions are correct, please don't wake me. After living my dream this long, I want to see how it all ends."

Does the place you're called to labor
Seem so small, and little known? . . .
Little is much when God is in it.
— *Little Is Much,* Kitty Suffield

25

The Summing Up

Though I have been blessed with wonderfully marvelous health and have missed only a few singing dates because of illness over the past thirty years, I was forced to take some time off not long ago because of an allergy reaction. While I was recuperating I made a trip to Syracuse, New York, where my mother, now eighty-seven, lives alone in a small apartment.

Still beautiful and full of life, Mother was even more solicitous than usual because of my slight malady. Like all mothers, I suppose, she looks upon her sons and daughters as children yet, and no amount of time will ever erase that image from her eyes.

One night I got to coughing and, try as I might, I could not muffle it enough to keep her from hearing. The predictable happened. First, there was a shuffle of slippers in her room, then noises in the kitchen — she was fixing something. Next came a knock at my door.

Pulling on my robe, I walked to the door and opened it. There, with the light from the kitchen framing her white hair like a halo, stood Mother with a cup of hot tea and a plate of her own oatmeal cookies. Seldom do I visit her but what she has baked cookies for me.

"Oh, Mother, you shouldn't have," I told her.

"Just drink this tea, Beverly," she put me down. "It will take care of that cough."

I pulled a chair up close to the bed for her, then sat down on the edge of the bed myself. After a couple of sips of tea, I said, "Just like old times, huh?"

Her face, covered with concern for me, warmed with a smile. "Yes, I've spent a few nights up with you and your brothers and sisters."

"Remember the days in Houghton when I missed all that school because of sickness?" I reminisced.

"Yes, and I tried to teach you in the kitchen . . . ." There was a pause and she stared out the window. But she wasn't looking at anything; it was still dark outside. No, she was thinking about some other days, long gone. My presence there, a boy with a cough, had triggered her thoughts and sent them reeling across the years.

Soon we were sharing some of our most poignant memories together. She remembered the time I dislodged Mr. Barnett's water pipe and flooded his barn. I reminded her of the time I fell in the creek while ice skating and returned home a walking cake of ice.

"Remember when Dad took me to the fair?"

"How could I forget," she sighed. "We had a long talk about that decision." One year in school I had been given an assignment to write an essay on some aspect of the local fair, which put me in a quandary because I had never been to a fair nor was I permitted to go. Because a fair always included a carnival with its games of chance, our church people did not normally attend.

When I asked him what was wrong with a fair, Dad looked at the ground a minute, stroking his chin. Then he looked up and said, "Get your coat, Beverly."

We walked in the main gate, right straight through the midway to the exhibition area. I had many questions to ask and he had answers for them all. It was not until I was much older, however, that I realized what a bold step Dad had taken. He had laid himself wide open to criticism from his parishioners — and all for me.

We recounted stories about old friends and acquaintances that night too. "Remember Harry Meeker's graduation speech?" I asked.

Mother threw up her hands in a gesture that said, "Who could forget Harry!"

Harry, one of the bubbling kind who never ran out of something to say, carved his name indelibly into my memory when he forgot his lines at one of the most dramatic parts of his speech. When his mind went blank, there was a long, embarrassing pause. Finally he broke the silence, "You know, folks, this subject grips me so." By the time the audience had stopped laughing, he had remembered his place and on he went, finishing in a flourish of forensic glory.

"I could have used his extemporaneous gift one night in the Cow Palace in San Francisco," I told Mother. The only difference between Harry's lapse and mine was that I forgot my lyrics in front of a few more thousand people.

"Did you see Kitty Suffield your last trip to California?" Mother inquired.

Kitty and Fred Suffield were the people who first got me up in front of an audience to sing in a tent meeting. Fred has died, but Kitty is still living in California. Though an invalid, she still has that wonderful outlook on life. I make it a point to call her whenever I'm in the area.

In 1963 during the Los Angeles Crusade, I took Kitty to the Coliseum for one of the services. I wheeled her to the elevator and took her to a spot in the Coliseum press box where she could see without being jostled by the crowd, which was more than 100,000. Before singing that night I told the audience that someone very special was present — someone who had written those beautiful hymns, "God Is Still on the Throne" and "Little Is Much." Then briefly I retold the story of her great contribution to my career and concluded by dedicating a song to her.

Mother remembered many other things . . . the revival service where I went forward . . . the move to Jersey City when Dad, Alton, and I went on ahead . . . the poem, "I'd Rather Have Jesus," which she placed on the old Bell piano for me to read . . . Dad's final sermon and the note we found at his death.

"I still have that paper," she said, "It was such a beautiful thought he left for us. So like him." Half to herself, half to me, she repeated the words:

> **Life has been wonderful,**
> **The promises of God precious,**
> **The eternal hope glorious.**

"God has blessed us in so many ways," Mother said, taking the thought from my mind and articulating it.

Then she got to her feet. "You need your rest, Son," she said, gathering up the dishes. "Can I get you something else?" She meant more tea or cookies, but I was thinking about other things.

"No, Mother," I responded. "You have given me *everything* I need."

I helped her to the kitchen with the dishes. Then she kissed me gently on the cheek and went into her room. In a minute the light went out and all was quiet. Quiet and dark — save for the light which glimmered unsteadily in from the street.

Though faint, it gave shape and color to the old Bell piano that sat just inside the next room. I walked into the room and ran my hands

over that family treasure. Without pressing hard enough to make a sound, I felt the keys.

Then reaching around to the side, I located the crack that Dad had closed after the piano had been damaged in the move to Houghton.

What a debt I owed that old instrument.

Through it, Mother had transmitted to me her love of music and faith in God. Through it, I first learned to express those stirrings inside me which sought release. Through it, I found my life's work, a way to tell others of Christ. Through it and the sacred song, I have known the mute to speak, the deaf to hear, the blind to see.

Sitting down on the piano bench, I bowed my head and recounted God's goodness to me. What a blessing it has been to be an instrument myself of His Good News. A small instrument, true. Just a simple psalm singer. Yet, if I have reached just one for Him, I am satisfied — satisfied and happy to be counted in that huge chorus cited in Longfellow's poem:

> **God sent His singers upon the earth**
> **With songs of sadness and of mirth,**
> **That they might touch the hearts of men,**
> **And bring them back to heaven again.**

— The Singers

From the Shea Family Album

I was fourteen and a high-school freshman in Ottawa, Canada, when this picture was taken. *Below:* How my gal Erma looked at seventeen, about the time I met her.

Erma had to make some repairs on her gown before this photograph could be snapped. I stepped on her hem as we left the altar.

I'D RATHER HAVE JESUS

Music by
GEORGE BEVERLY SHEA

Copyright 1967, Chancel Music, Inc.

Twenty (but not in this picture) when I wrote the tune for "I'd Rather Have Jesus," over a million copies of the sheet music have been distributed. *(BGEA Photo by Russ Busby) Below:* Teammates—we worked together for the first time in 1947 in Charlotte, North Carolina. Left to right, Grady Wilson, GBS, Billy Graham and Cliff Barrows.

At one time, I was quite a photography buff. I caught this shot of twenty-nine-year-old Billy in Albuquerque. *Below:* A hymn sing in Nashville. With me, left to right, Homer Rodeheaver, who sang with Billy Sunday; Wally Fowler and Frank Clement, former governor of Tennessee. (*Jack House photo*)

My first RCA Victor recording session in the New York studio, with the Hugo Winterhalter Orchestra.

The reed organ, the "kist o' whustles" Ira Sankey used to introduce "The Ninety and Nine." I first saw this organ in Scotland, when we visited there in 1949 for *Youth for Christ*. Later, it was given to the Billy Graham Evangelistic Association and is now kept in Minneapolis.

Two doctors: The real one, Stephen Paine, president of Houghton College, is on the left. The honorary doctorate was presented to me in 1956. *(Preston Studio, Belmont, N. Y.)*

This was the Presidential Prayer Breakfast in 1954, at which I was asked to lead the audience in "What A Friend We Have in Jesus." On the dais, left to right: Chief Justice Earl Warren, Conrad Hilton, President Dwight D. Eisenhower, Abraham Vereide, E. J. Mack, Senator Frank Carlson and Vice President Richard M. Nixon.

On tour in England in 1962 with Tedd Smith. One of the highlights of the trip was the warm reception we received at London's Royal Albert Hall. This concert was attended by 7,800 people I'm told, 800 of whom were standing. *(Photo-Reportage, Ltd., London)*

Bobby Richardson Day at Yankee Stadium. It was Bobby's request that I sing "How Great Thou Art," and I was only too happy to oblige. He is one great guy. (*Gospel Films, Inc., Photo*)

In Hollywood at a little party given for me by the RCA people in 1966. The occasion was held to mark the sale of my one millionth album. Presenting a trophy to me is Neely Plumb while Darol Rice, my A & R man, left, and John K. West look on.

On the platform, this time at the Chicago Crusade in McCormack Place. *Below:* A panoramic shot of the Los Angeles Coliseum, November, 1963. This was the climax of the Southern California Crusade attended by 134,000 people.

Vietnam, December 24, 1966. A driving rain didn't keep these soldiers, part of Operation Hammond, from attending our service. *(U.S. Air Force photo)* The shot at right is of Billy and me in Saigon.